life is
Messy

BLUE SPARROW
North Palm Beach, Florida

MATTHEW KELLY

BLUE
sparrow

Copyright © 2021
KAKADU, LLC
PUBLISHED BY BLUE SPARROW

ISBN: 978-1-63582-200-7 (hardcover)
ISBN: 978-1-63582-201-4 (e-book)

Designed by Ashley Dias

10   9   8   7   6   5   4   3   2

FIRST EDITION

Printed in the United States of America

Contents

"There's no limit to how complicated things can get on account of one thing always leading to another."

- E.B. White,
from *Charlotte's Web*

The human dilemma.

Life is messy.

This is the human dilemma. You're not doing it wrong.

Life isn't a color-within-the-lines exercise. It's a wild and outrageous invitation full of uncertain outcomes. Sometimes it is beautifully rational, at other times it lacks all logic. What appears to be a step back today, may turn out to be the first marvelous step forward ten years from now.

The mess of life is both inevitable and unexpected. It is filled with delightful mysteries and frustrating predicaments, indescribable joy and heart-wrenching suffering.

There is no plan you can devise that will solve the mess. There is nothing you can buy, learn, or accomplish that will eliminate the mess. Finding the love of your life and the perfect career won't either. There is nothing you can start doing or stop doing that will eradicate the mess. There's nothing you can tell yourself that will make the mess magically disappear, and you cannot think your way out of it. The mess is here to stay. It's unavoidable. It's just life.

It's what we do with the mess that determines everything. You can ignore it, avoid it, deny it, blame others, shame yourself, and exhaust yourself pretending your life isn't messy. But when you wake tomorrow morning, the mess will still be there. Or you can realize that the mess serves a powerful purpose.

To discover that powerful purpose, we first need to accept that the mess is not the problem. The problem is our erroneous belief that everything should be immaculate, orderly, neat, tidy, and in its place.

Everyone has their own mess to contend with. Our tendency is to think that we are the only ones with a mess, that our mess is messier, more embarrassing, more shameful than other people's mess. It isn't so.

You don't have to it have it all together. Nobody has it all together.

Acceptance is the only way to make peace with the mess. This acceptance will lead you to a profound acceptance of life, others, and self. It isn't surrender or defeat. It isn't conceding that there is nothing we can do about the mess. It's just a penetrating awareness that the meaning of life isn't to solve the mess. That's not the goal.

This radical acceptance of self, others, and life may be the beginning of wisdom. I'm not sure we can ever truly appreciate anyone or anything until we have made peace with the mess. Are you ready to make peace with the mess?

Life is messy, but we figure things out. We laugh, we cry, we grow, and we move on to new beginnings, second chances, and amazing possibilities.

A more beautiful question.

The gateway between confusion and clarity is marked with a quintessential truth: We are wounded and broken. Acceptance of this truth allows us to make peace with the mess.

I am wounded and broken. We all are. We are self-conscious

about our brokenness. We are sensitive and insecure, even embarrassed, about our woundedness. But we needn't be. We are all wounded and broken.

Why are we so surprised when we discover that another person is broken? Perhaps because we are so intent on ignoring our own brokenness. Everyone is broken, everyone is wounded, to pretend otherwise is to open ourselves to vast and ongoing deception.

But it's okay that we are broken. It's only a problem if we subscribe to the false notion that we have to try to keep everyone and everything from being broken.

I am broken. Pretending otherwise is exhausting.

But let me share with you the real problem with our brokenness. In our wasteful, consumption-addicted society, we throw broken things away. So, we don't know what to do with our broken selves. What do we do with broken people, broken relationships, broken institutions, broken families, and of course, our very own broken selves?

This is an important question, but a more beautiful question holds the answer. It is one of the most beautiful questions I have ever stumbled upon: Can something that has been broken be put back together in a way that makes it more beautiful than ever before?

This is the question that all the words on these pages cling to.

It may seem like an impossible proposition to our straight-line, everything-in-its-place, secular minds. But I marvel at how God doesn't use straight lines or right-angles in nature. We invented right-angles and straight lines to prop up our insecure humanity.

The perfection of nature is marked by crooked lines, brokenness, imperfect colors, and things that seem out of place. The perfection of creation is achieved through its imperfection. And so it is with human beings. Your imperfections are part of what make you perfectly yourself.

If we put on the mind of God, we discover one of the most beautiful truths this life has to offer: Something that has been devastatingly broken can be put back together in a way that makes it more beautiful than ever before. It is true for things, but it is even more true for people, and it is true for you. This is the source and the summit of hope.

We believe that once something is broken it can never be as beautiful as it was before. But that's not true. It's true that it cannot be exactly the same as it was before, but that doesn't mean it cannot surpass its former self. You don't look at a wonderful tree that loses some leaves and limbs in a storm, and say, "It's ruined forever." But we say that about ourselves and others.

The Japanese have a beautiful artform called Kintsugi. It is a form of ceramics, and I have been meditating on it for the past several years. In our disposable culture, if we break a vase or a bowl, we throw it away and buy a new one. This simple act allows us to maintain the illusion that life is not messy. It plays into our delusion of perfection. But life is messy, perfect is a myth, and the wisdom of the Japanese art of Kintsugi has much to teach us.

When a vase or bowl or cup is broken, artists gather up the broken pieces and glue them back together. Though it is how they put them back together that is steeped in wisdom and beauty. They mix gold dust with the glue. They don't try to hide the cracks. They own them, honor them, even accentuate them by making them golden. They celebrate the cracks as part of their story.

This is a beautiful lesson. They don't pretend the vase was never broken. They don't pretend that life is not messy. They don't pretend they are not broken. When we pretend to be someone other than who we are, our true self hides in fear and shame; the fear of being discovered and the shame of not being enough.

The most beautiful and surprising lesson the Kintsugi art-form teaches us is this: We are each other's wounded healers. *We each possess the gold dust needed to glue other people back together, making them more beautiful and loveable than ever.* Our love, connection, acceptance, generosity, community, and kindness are that gold dust. This is astoundingly profound.

There is a vital truth here. Kintsugi ceramics are staggeringly beautiful. There is an honesty to their beauty that is missing in the artificial perfection of mass-produced items. Once repaired in this ancient method, Kintsugi pieces are more beautiful, and more loved than before they were broken.

This idea creates vast confusion and cognitive resistance

for us. We don't believe that something that has been broken and repaired can be more beautiful, and more loved, than ever before. But hope depends on overcoming this false belief. Moving on from this false assumption is essential to making peace with our own brokenness and a vital ingredient in all healthy relationships.

Someone who has been broken and healed can be more beautiful, and more loved, than ever before. Embracing this truth is liberating. But it is easier to do once we realize it's okay to be broken. It's normal, in fact—part of the human condition. Once we embrace this truth, we are on the path of hope. When we reject it, we are on the road to despair.

Can someone who has been broken be healed and become more beautiful and more lovable than ever before?

This is the central question in our journey together. I am convinced the answer to the question is yes. But as you will soon discover, arriving at this conviction was no easy feat. This book is my own messy and imperfect grappling with this question. If at any point in this book you find yourself lost, confused, or disoriented, return to this question. It is the North Star we are exploring. Whatever topic we are discussing in the pages ahead, though they are vast and varied, we will never be far from this question.

Someone who has been broken and healed *can* become more beautiful and more lovable than ever before. That someone is you. My singular hope as you make your way through these pages is that you discover this to be true.

Inadequate.

These pages were born out of three years of excruciating suffering. There are no words for what I experienced. Even words dripping with meaning leave so much unsaid. But words are all I have. They are my craft. I am a wordsmith, a smithy of words, and so, I have done the best I know how.

The easiest thing would have been not to write about this period of my life. I was tempted to set aside the journals that much of this content was drawn from and never revisit them. But they kept calling to me, so it is my hope that this whole mess will serve you in some way that is unknowable to me.

Writing makes me feel inadequate. It's one of those things that you never quite get right. I know I can never get down on paper what I see with the eyes of my soul. And still, I try. It is a most glorious frustration. Most days I feel like a dedicated but clumsy translator, trying desperately to translate what I experience, feel, hope, and observe. There are times when I feel like I am so close, only to wake up the next morning, read yesterday's pages, and discover I am still so far away. If you have ever felt inadequate, unequal to the task at hand, deficient in any way, then you know how I feel—and I thank you for your grace and understanding.

Still, it's the possibilities that draw me forward. The possibility of love, community, greater meaning, connection with others, all the firsts and lasts of life, old friends and new adventures. And the possibility that I might write something that stirs your soul.

This isn't like other books I have written. It's messy. I haven't tried to smooth out the rough edges. It doesn't start and end neatly. There are no chapters or parts. Each section is unto itself. I wrote them for myself, at different times in different places, never expecting that anyone else would read them. You will be able to tell which parts were written during my times of trauma, which were written to help me move forward, and which are reflecting on those times in my life. I have made no effort to hide that. Though I have tried to organize them loosely into a journey for you, and I have adjusted the original journal language in most parts to address the reader. Some of the transitions from one section to the next are rough. In my journals, those rough transitions wake me up and force me to pay attention when I re-read them, so I have decided to keep them.

Leonardo da Vinci observed, "Art is never finished, only abandoned." And so, I abandon this book to you now, hoping that somehow, imperfect and inadequate as it is, it will speak to you wherever you are in your journey and open your heart to undiscovered possibilities . . .

The worst year of my life.

Everything was fine until everything wasn't.

We are never ready for the storms of life. They rarely announce themselves. These storms come at unexpected times and in unexpected forms. They come in all shapes and sizes, and teach us that life is unpredictable and messy. You can search for shelter from the storm, but sometimes there is none to be found, and you find yourself completely exposed. Some of life's storms are mild enough that you can make the best of them and dance in the rain. But others are so violent that they knock the wind out of you, leaving you gasping for air and questioning everything.

Between Thanksgiving and Christmas each year I work through a series of exercises that help me reflect on the year that has been and plan for the year to come. The process has evolved over the past thirty years, but I have always begun with this question: Has this been the best year of my life so far?

For decades I had an extraordinary run—magical, really. One year had been better than the other, and the next year better than that. The answer to the question year after year was a resounding YES! Until a few years ago, when the answer was NO! I didn't have to think about it. It was clear. It wasn't even close. The answer was unequivocally no. This was uncharted territory. It was the first time in my life this had happened. It wasn't just that the past year had failed to outshine the year prior. It had been the worst year of my life.

I reflected upon it. Analyzed my part in it. Considered the roles other people had played. Hoped it was an anomaly. Optimistically explored how I could overcome this *slump* and made plans to turn it around. *It* being my life.

This didn't work. The following year was worse again. The slump continued, deepened, and I set another record for the worst year of my life. I was headed in the wrong direction and I was afraid. When something happens once, it's an event. When something happens twice, it becomes a pattern.

Disappointed but not broken, I retrieved some lingering hope from the depths of my being, bandaged up my battered ego, and put together a new plan to restore the trajectory of my life.

That didn't work either. Actually, it's not that it didn't work, but that all hell broke loose in my life. Literally. In that third year I saw the worst of many people. In just twelve short months, I was deceived and betrayed by so many people, in so many ways, that I became at times stunned, enraged, disoriented, and depressed.

Betrayal awakens you with such a jolt. It electrifies you in such a way that you are not sure you will ever fall asleep again. And yet, all you want to do is sleep. You hope you will wake and discover it was all just a dream. But you can't sleep. And it is not a dream. This nightmare is your life now.

The dark side of humanity came to visit me, not in one situation, but in a series of plagues. Some I brought upon myself and others were inflicted upon me. Some I have come to understand and some I may never. Some I have recovered from and others have me lying awake some nights wondering if I ever will.

For better and for worse, they have shaped the man I am today. I would like to say that I allowed each of these experiences to make me a better person, but I cannot, and I refuse to pretend. It's just too exhausting.

Some of the experiences leave me sad, others leave me disappointed and heartbroken, there are some that make me hungry for revenge, some just leave me a little jaded, and I have allowed others to make me more cynical than I would like. It was a season of tragedy and betrayal in my life, and I will never be the same. The most difficult of these experiences have left me deeply wounded—so wounded, that some days, I stare at my scars in disbelief, and I wonder how wounds so brutal didn't kill me.

What did I do wrong?

This was the question I kept asking myself: What did I do wrong? It's sick, but I think I wanted to blame myself. I ruminated on this question for weeks and months, and ruminating on the ways you have been wronged is unhealthy. Still, I kept pondering the question, over and over again. But there are no answers to some questions. At least no answers that will satisfy us. One question answered gives birth to five more questions.

One of life's enduring mysteries is that you don't have to do anything wrong for your life to go horribly wrong. When we are abused, rejected, hurt, betrayed, or manipulated, we search our hearts and minds, wondering what we did wrong. Maybe you did things to open or close doors, but it is not your fault.

People make choices and they hurt us, but it's not our fault. Don't take it personally. I know it sounds ridiculous, but it's profoundly true. When a man breaks up with a woman and says, "It's not you, it's me," unconsciously he's being outrageously honest. The drunk who says, "I wasn't thinking" isn't lying. She wasn't thinking about her husband and children. The man who cheats on his wife and says he didn't think about how it would affect his wife and children isn't lying. When we get in these self-destructive places, we are so self-absorbed that we don't think of anyone or anything else. That's why they call it selfishness.

Unexpected.

Life didn't turn out the way I expected. In some ways it has exceeded my expectations, and in other ways it has disappointed them. Never in my wildest dreams as a child would I have imagined the life I have lived. The adventures, experiences, and opportunities, the love I have given and received, and the success I have enjoyed have all far exceeded my expectations. But I also never imagined in my worst nightmares the dark side of these bright lights.

We all end up living unexpected lives.

There are hopes and dreams that didn't materialize that I grieve, but I have been surprised and delighted by other unexpected gifts. And there are hopes and dreams that I am glad did not come to fruition. The unexpected goes both ways.

But these are not the things that make life most unexpected. It's the truly unexpected things, those we don't hope for or fear—particularly those that come out of nowhere and break our hearts. You wake up one morning and discover that your life has been changed forever, because of something you did or something someone else did. It's the things we don't plan, the things we never imagined would happen. It's those unexpected events that slap you so hard in the face that you can taste blood in your mouth.

Nobody's life turns out the way they expect it to. We shouldn't be surprised. Nobody looks back on life to discover it unfolded exactly as they hoped or planned, but I found myself particularly unprepared for the inevitability of the unexpected. That's the paradox: It is inevitable that we live unexpected lives.

Life doesn't unfold according to our plans. But sooner or later, we each have to decide how we are going to make the most of our one, brief, unexpected life. It is then that we come face-to-face with two enduring truths: We cannot live without hope that things will change for the better, and we are not victims of our circumstances.

Hope is not always as accessible as we would like. It often seems just out of reach at those times when we are most in need of it, when our hearts are broken, our minds downtrodden, and our souls crushed. Yet, even in those moments, we have a choice. The unexpected is either a curse or an opportunity. We get to decide.

When your reality becomes a nightmare.

Sometimes life just hurts. I knew I was in a dark place when my thoughts during the day were as disquieting as the

13

nightmares I was having at night. What's the point of waking from a nightmare when what you wake to is the reality of the nightmare?

There were mornings I would wake to a moment of relief. I would think, *It's okay, it was just a bad dream.* But then my hope would be demolished as I wiped the sleep from my eyes and realized it wasn't just a dream. This was my life now. I didn't know if sleep was my friend or my enemy. Sometimes it was hard to know where the nightmare ended and reality began.

Pain, trauma, and grief distort time. I would tell myself, "This is not a dream. It's not even a nightmare. This is my life." But that wasn't true. I would say to myself, "No. This is your life *right now.*" And just adding those two words—*right now*—changes everything. It may be your life right now, but that doesn't mean it will be your life forever.

Still, you relive things in your mind. And reliving them re-traumatizes you. But you can't help yourself. You wonder if you could go back—which of course you can't—but if by some magic or miracle you could have a mulligan in this one situation, would you have done it differently. You mull it over in your mind, consider a thousand ways that it could have gone differently, and still, you are where you are. That's the thing about the scariest carnival rides—you end up where you started. But reliving these things over and over again in your mind is no way to live.

It's one thing if you brought the situation upon yourself. We often do. But if you didn't, these ruminations become even more fruitless as you realize that even if you could go back, you were not the actor. You were acted upon. You were not the cause; your suffering is the effect. It was caused by someone else's choice. Many other people, perhaps. And, even if you could go back, you could change what you did and said, but you couldn't change what they said and did.

And then it dawns on you, again: There is no solution. We are so used to fixing things and solving problems that it seems unbelievable at first. But after we go through the situation in our minds a few hundred times, we realize that this is not one of Edison's experiments, in which each failure gets you closer to success. You realize this is your life and there simply are no solutions to some problems. Some of life's unnatural disasters you just have to live with and hope the pain fades over time.

Will the hurt ever stop?

There was another question that kept returning: Will the hurt ever stop? While the storm of suffering was still raging, I would think about horrible things I had endured in the past and remind myself that at those times I thought I would never get beyond those situations, but I did.

It was of little consolation. This felt different. It was of a different magnitude. The night was darker than it had ever been, and even daylight, the sun on my face, hurt some days. I can't describe what it felt like, but I could see what it was doing to me. And I didn't like it.

The problem with this kind of pain is that it stops you

from enjoying almost everything. It overshadows everything. There's a brilliant line in one of James Taylors songs: *The secret of life is enjoying the passage of time.* He dispenses this wisdom so casually. But this is exactly what you can't do when you have been hurt deeply. When you have been traumatized you cannot enjoy the passage of time. Like a dog that's been beaten, you flinch at life, afraid that anything or anyone, at any moment, could re-traumatize you.

There are some things that happen in our lives that hurt so deeply that we spend weeks and months of our lives wondering if we will ever stop hurting. The pain will eventually subside, but we don't know that at the time. Depending on what caused the pain, it may never go away completely, but over time its intensity diminishes.

The pain subsides. When something subsides, by definition, it becomes less intense, less violent, less severe. This of course means that it was intense, violent, and severe to begin with. And something subsiding is not the same as something going away. There is pain that has no end. If we live long enough, it seems, we all experience such pain.

There are nights when you can't fall asleep. Your mind ruminates. You hope for sleep, plead and pray for relief, but then when you sleep there are the nightmares. There were days when I would wake up and grief would be standing right beside my bed, waiting to kick me in the stomach. There were days when I would wake and curl up in a ball, incapable of getting out of bed. Other days I forced myself to get up only to crawl helplessly back into bed after taking a step or two. The pain was unimaginable, the torment indescribable. It was a blinding relentless pain that causes you to forget there was ever a life without it.

There is a haunting line in the musical *Les Misérables*: *There's a grief that can't be spoken. There's a pain goes on and on.* It's true. There is a grief that seems all-encompassing. It seems like it never ends. It robs you of all your yesterdays and tomorrows. When you are in the grip of grief, everyone and everything reminds you of your loss. You feel raw and exposed. Naked in a world with no clothes. Fragile and defenseless.

Will it always be this bad? I wondered. *Will it always hurt this much?* I hoped not.

When you have a soul-crushing experience, it's the first thing you think of every morning when you wake. Until it isn't. Out of nowhere, one day, I don't know when or how, comes miraculous relief. On that day, your loss is the second thing you think about. And then, more time passes, and it's the third thing you think about each day.

The days fade into weeks, the weeks blur into months. You begin to desperately hope that you have found a way to live with your grief. Then one day, you're going about your day, doing what you do, and out of nowhere, grief slaps you in the face so hard you are sure one of your teeth has come loose. What triggered it? A trifle. The slightest thing. A song, a photo, a memory, a word, a phrase, a place, a smell. Anything can set it off.

Grief is like a bear. It retreats to its cave, sometimes for long periods, and then one day you turn around and discover that the bear has crept up behind you. It scares you half to death. The fright re-traumatizes you. It can be crippling. But then the bear wanders back into the cave to hibernate again. When will it return? Nobody knows. Grief doesn't make appointments. It has its own timetable.

But grief is your friend. It may not seem like it, but it's helping you heal. It's a mistake to pretend it isn't there. It is so easy to become embarrassed or ashamed of grief. This is also a mistake. Have no shame in your grief. Allow it to wash over you. Invite it to heal you. Just know that while there will be times when the enormity of your grief seems insurmountable, you are more than your grief. Be gentle with yourself. Be patient with yourself.

These are the things I told myself, the things I wrote in my journal. Some days they helped and some days they didn't.

Feelings.

Feelings are visitors of the heart. Welcome them. Each feeling comes to teach you something very specific. Be hospitable to these guests. They are only passing through. Unless you ignore them. This detains them unnecessarily. You cannot get them to leave by ignoring them, avoiding them, or pretending they don't exist. They will stay until you attend to them. And when it comes time for them to leave, thank them for visiting.

Wait it out.

There are some situations in life that need to be dealt with. They require action. There are other things in life that we simply need to wait out. This can be excruciatingly difficult. It is much easier to do something, anything, than it is to patiently do nothing.

Knowing when to act and when to wait something out begins simply by being aware that there are two options. Our instinct is to act; we have a bias toward action. This bias blinds us to every other possibility. We often don't even consider doing nothing as an option. Bold action is beautiful when action is what is needed. Any action is clumsy when what is needed is inaction.

Learning to wait things out is one of life's greatest lessons, and it can be learned only by waiting things out. Sometimes the wisest thing to do is nothing, it is also often the hardest thing to do.

One of the worst nights of my life was in my twenties. At that time, I was traveling and speaking all the time. Two hundred and fifty days a year began in an airport. Sometimes more. A few months earlier I had released a new book, and suddenly there was a lot of media interest in Australia. My Australian publisher had asked me to visit. "We just need you on the ground for forty-eight hours," I can remember them saying. So, we squeezed a trip into an already insane schedule. I have that awareness now, but I didn't at the time. Sometimes you don't realize how insane something is until you stop doing it.

I flew from Miami to Los Angeles and on to Sydney. I worked two very long days and then flew from Sydney to Los Angeles, and on to Pittsburgh. I was living not far from Pittsburgh at the time. When I got to bed that night, I had crossed forty-four time zones in less than four days.

Now, jet lag is real. There are people who think it's a myth. Maybe they have a unique constitution, or maybe they have never travelled enough to experience it. But if you are taking a long trip, my advice is to take it seriously. The effects of jet lag are dehydration, difficulty focusing, inability to function at work, feeling disoriented and confused, extreme fatigue, trouble falling asleep, trouble staying asleep, trouble waking up, falling asleep in the middle of the day, moodiness, gastrointestinal issues, and a general feeling of being unwell. Experts say it can take as long as one day per time zone crossed to recover your normal circadian rhythms. That means it could take up to forty-four days to recover from the trip I had just taken.

When I landed in Pittsburgh, I had an urgent message from my girlfriend in San Francisco. When I called, she was clearly upset and said she needed to see me as soon as possible. "What's happened?" I asked. "I don't want to talk about it on the phone," she answered, "Can you come here?"

It was eleven o'clock at night and I was still waiting at baggage claim for my bag. I walked upstairs to the ticket counter and booked a seat on the six a.m. flight to San Francisco the next morning. I went home, but I couldn't sleep. Came back to the airport, boarded the plane for the West Coast, and fell asleep at some point during the flight. We had landed and taxied to the gate, and every other passenger was off the flight when the flight attendant woke me. I was oblivious. It was eight a.m. on the West Coast.

"Let's meet for breakfast," my girlfriend said when I called to let her know I had landed. So, I took a taxi to Mama's on Washington Square and waited for her to arrive.

When she arrived, she ordered coffee but nothing to eat. She then told me she had decided to get back together with an old boyfriend from years ago, that she was breaking up with me, but hadn't wanted to do it on the phone.

I was in a daze. I thought someone had died, or that she had lost her job, or that something else terrible had happened. We hadn't been dating long enough to warrant the insanity of me getting back on a plane after the trip I had just had. After the trip *she knew* I had just had. I wasn't heartbroken, I was stunned. I wasn't angry that she had gone back to her old boyfriend, I was angry that she had summoned me across the country.

The fog lifted. My focus shifted from my own self-pity to her restlessness. Something wasn't right. There was more to the story. I sensed she wanted to talk, but for some reason she was holding back. I asked if everything else was okay. I asked if something else was troubling her. But nothing. I couldn't get her to open up. I couldn't even get her gaze to meet my eyes.

A few minutes later she left. I took a taxi to a hotel by the airport and on the way called to book a flight for the next morning. It was still early. I could have flown straight home, but I desperately needed to sleep.

Closing the curtains, I blacked out the hotel room; the red numbers on the clock read 11:07 a.m. I slept. For three hours. Then I tossed and turned for a couple of hours before accepting that I was not about to fall back to sleep anytime soon. I was confused and disoriented. I kept going over various scenarios in my mind. It just didn't make sense. It was like trying to put together a jigsaw puzzle without all the pieces.

I have had some long days, weeks, and months working under enormous deadlines. But I don't think I had ever been so tired in my life. I went for a walk, did a little work, tried to eat something, and went back to bed.

That was one of the longest nights of my life. I was miserable. I couldn't sleep. I was baffled by the events of the day. It was a lonely time in my life. I wanted to talk to someone, but I didn't know what I wanted to talk about. It wasn't the girl. It was something more, something bigger. I was beyond exhausted, and that place is a wasteland for the heart, mind, and soul. It felt like I was going mad. I was in pain, but I didn't know where it hurt. It wasn't physical pain; it was existential pain. There were moments that night when I wished I was dead. I didn't think about hurting myself. I just wanted that pain to stop. I needed to sleep, but sleep refused to come.

There are some moments in our lives that are so pivotal that we never stop drawing on them for wisdom, courage, and direction. That night was one of them for me. I don't know what I was in the grips of that night. But I do know it taught me one of life's most powerful lessons: Sometimes all you can do is wait it out.

It took me years to actualize the wisdom of that night. I didn't know I was having a touchstone moment. Looking back across the years, I am glad for the experience. There have been many more unpleasant experiences I have had to endure, some considerably worse than what I experienced that night. I often find myself reflecting on that night in San Francisco. "All you have to do is wait it out," I say to myself. "You don't have to do anything. Just wait patiently and let it pass."

That night taught me something else. Every night when you and I get into bed, our day is ending, but somewhere, others are facing the longest night of their lives. When you're struggling to survive your harshest night, hopelessness can so easily take a hold. So, as I lay my head on my pillow, I whisper a prayer for the men, women, and children whose long dark night is just beginning.

I never heard from the girl again. But fifteen years later, I learned that when she sat down to breakfast that morning, she was pregnant. Looking back the pieces fall into place.

When nothing makes sense.

It only takes one event to send life into a tailspin. A single event can completely blindside you and leave you feeling disoriented. Something happens and suddenly nothing makes sense anymore. You stagger around in shock and disbelief.

It's like discovering that water isn't wet or that one plus one doesn't equal two.

We expect life to unfold in certain ways. We expect our relationships, careers, and personal finances to follow paths that we have constructed in our minds. We expect health, not sickness. We expect a long life, not a short one. We expect prosperity, not poverty. We expect to be respected, not disrespected.

Some of our expectations are more aligned with reality than others. The unreasonable expectations we have of ourselves and other people will lead to either wisdom or pain. If we examine our expectations and dismantle those that are false and unreasonable, they can be transmuted into a rare form of wisdom. If on the other hand, we stubbornly hold onto our unreasonable expectations, reality will demolish them, and we will suffer.

I was experiencing the latter. Reality was dismantling my illusions and destroying my unrealistic expectations. And it was all happening so quickly. I woke up one morning and before I went to bed that night my whole life had changed forever. And it happened more than once. Several times. It's no wonder I felt disoriented.

The interesting thing is that positive and negative events can be equally disorienting. The negative side is easier to comprehend. We expect negative experiences to disquiet our soul. The death of a parent, friend, child, or spouse. Losing your job. Loneliness and isolation. Being abused. Divorce.

Being told by your doctor that you have a life-threatening disease. Infidelity. Depression. A sick child. A loveless marriage. Being arrested. A miscarriage. Missed opportunity. War. A natural disaster. Terrorism. Addiction. Discrimination. A car accident. Insurmountable debt. Being robbed. These events may be a surprise, but how they affect us usually isn't.

What's surprising is that positive events can stir our souls in different but equally unsettling ways.

You go on a long-anticipated vacation only to discover as you lie on the beach that your life no longer makes sense to you. The perspective of a little time away causes you to realize that you have deprioritized what matters most.

You get engaged only to discover that the time leading up to the wedding can be among the most stressful times in your life.

You move into your dream home, but the stress of the transition reveals things about the role you allow material possessions to play in your life.

You give birth to a child and this new life puts everything you have ever experienced in a new context. Your love for this child rearranges your priorities and you know you can never go back. The old you seems foreign. You don't recognize her. It's as if that was a completely different person.

You look forward to retirement and doing whatever you want, whenever you want, only to discover after just a few months that it is a deeply unsatisfying experience.

Life can be disorienting. It can happen quickly. And this

disorientation can be brought on by either a positive or negative event. It can lead to a shift in priorities, but not always. Sometimes we repress our new discoveries about self and life. Disorientation is an invitation.

It's a mistake to focus on the negative. It's a mistake sometimes to think the bad stuff is all bad. It is often in the middle of nowhere, lost and confused, when nothing makes sense, that we find ourselves and come to know ourselves in new and brilliant ways.

Sometimes when your life has been turned upside down, after the dust settles, you discover that your life is finally right side up. Sometimes when you feel lost you are exactly where you need to be at that moment.

The question is: Can getting lost be a good thing? Do you view getting lost as inconvenient, frustrating, an adventure, or an opportunity? The answer is different for every person in every situation, but most of the time when we get lost, we don't even consider some of these options. Maybe getting lost is exactly what we need.

Dante's truth.

The Italian poet and moral philosopher of the thirteenth-century, Dante Alighieri, knew more than most just how messy life and our shared humanity can be at times. He opens his epic work *The Divine Comedy* with these words. Writing over seven hundred years ago, Dante knew just how lost and disoriented we all become at times in life.

"In the middle of the journey of our life I found myself in a dark woods where the straight way had been lost sight of. How hard it is to say what it was like in the thick of thickets, in a wood so dense and gnarled the very thought of it renews my panic. It is bitter almost as death itself is bitter. But to rehearse the good it also brought me I will speak about the other things I saw there. How I got there I cannot clearly say, for I was moving like a sleepwalker the moment I stepped out of the right way."

I have been in these woods that Dante described. I have been there more than once. He describes finding himself lost in the dark woods. When we find ourselves lost, we tend to think of it as a crisis. The reality is it can be a crisis or an opportunity. We get to decide. But this opportunity is not to be squandered. Immersed in these fires, we can learn more about ourselves in one year than any other ten years of our lives.

Dante says so much in these few lines. It was the middle of his journey. He was in the dark. He had lost sight of the straight path. He didn't recognize where he was. It was like nothing he had known, so much so, that he could not rightly describe it other than to say it was like a dense wood. So thick he was in a panic. He likens it to death, but points out that good things came from it. He didn't know how he got there, but was aware that he had been walking unconsciously. And he knew he had stepped off the right path.

How do we know if we are experiencing these dark woods

Dante describes? There are many signs, and everyone's experience is different. But some of the signs are: you begin asking deep probing questions; you lose interest in the things you were once passionate about; nothing seems to make sense; the future seems particularly unclear or uncertain, or the future you see seems especially unattractive or meaningless to you; you have trouble sleeping through the night or all you want to do is sleep; you have become generally restless; you become apathetic, everything seems vanilla; you start behaving recklessly; or you are unusually envious of other people.

The first lesson of the dark woods is that life is messy. Some people respond by saying to themselves, "Well, things are already a mess, I might as well make some more mess and the types of mess I have always fantasized about." Other people respond by trying to exile their mess. They get new friends, a new job, and new stuff. They tell themselves they are starting a whole new life, free from all the mess of their past. They forget the inescapable mess that is within.

There is wisdom in the mess. Immerse yourself in the wisdom of the mess with all the courage and consciousness you can muster. How? Acknowledge that life is messy. Realize that we are all wounded and broken. Accept some level of responsibility for your mess. This acknowledgement, realization, and acceptance are the prerequisites for the wisdom of a messy life. Together they give birth to a piercing awareness of how we came to be where we are and what we need to do to continue our journey.

The dark night of the soul.

In the sixteenth-century, a Spanish mystic named John of the Cross penned a poem known as *Dark Night of the Soul*. It narrates the journey of the soul and marks one of the most significant spiritual discoveries of all time.

The dark night of the soul is a spiritual crisis, a form of spiritual depression, an existential quandary. It produces doubt, confusion, and soul sadness. The soul sadness we experience during the dark night is an extreme form of sadness that has no cause or explanation. It also produces a spiritual condition known as desolation. In this state you experience the anguish of complete emptiness. Everything seems meaningless. John of the Cross describes being "lost in oblivion."

The dark night of the soul annihilates anything you believe about yourself that is not true. Everything is stripped away except your essential self. Your old self is left behind and your new self emerges. And when the darkness lifts, you have clarity like never before, because all that is left is the self you cannot live without and a piercing sense of how to spend the rest of your life.

Emptiness.

There have been moments of unbelievable abundance in my life, but I have also experienced moments of staggering emptiness. And at this time, I was experiencing a moment of profound emptiness. I had been here before, but never like this. Imagine being hungry and wondering if you will ever have your fill ever again. Not that you will die of starvation, but that you will be hungry for the rest of your life. That's how I was feeling.

The thing is the emptiness cannot be dealt with once and for all. There are times in life when we feel so satisfied, so full, brimming and overflowing. One of my most vivid memories of contentment and happiness was just after my daughter was born. I was laying on the bed next to her, she was smiling and making baby noises, and I was suddenly overcome by a wave of endless gratitude. I kept hearing that line from Lou Gehrig's speech at Yankee Stadium over and over in my mind: "Today I consider myself the luckiest man on the face of the earth." I was so happy I started to cry. It was one of the highest highs of my life. But in the weeks ahead a series of events unfolded so quickly they gave me spiritual whiplash. Life went from record highs to record lows in breakneck speed. And once again I found myself experiencing a profound emptiness, and wondering, how can such nothingness be so consuming?

We all experience emptiness, and we all have ways of dealing with it. I have dealt with emptiness throughout my life in a variety of ways. They have all been equally ineffective, except one.

I have tried to fill the void with work, pleasure, comfort, things, and plans for the future. But none of these bring satisfaction because these things don't rightfully belong in the void. When I am finished distracting myself with these things the emptiness is still there.

There is only one approach that has ever worked consistently. I know it works, but still, I resist it, preferring these other distractions to the real solution. We all share in this insanity. If we observe ourselves in these moments, we gain unique insight into the mess. Every day we encounter moments of decision. The better path is clear, but we choose another path. The better path leads to the destination we wish to arrive at, and still, we choose another path. Each time we choose another path, our lives become messier.

Learning to deal with our emptiness in a healthy way is one thing. Choosing to deal with emptiness in a healthy way requires self-awareness and courage. The difference between learning and choosing is akin to the difference between knowledge and wisdom.

I have only found one way that works. This is it. Find a quiet place, sit down, close your eyes, acknowledge God's presence, breathe deeply, talk to him briefly about how life has left you empty, and ask God to fill you.

I know. It sounds so simple. Too simple. But the simplicity or complexity is irrelevant. All that matters is this: Does it work?

Why is life so messy?

It's a reasonable question. But it's worth asking whether we really want to know the answer. Perhaps we already know the answer, but we ask the question, hoping that maybe, somehow, the answer will be different.

Life is messy because I am messy. It's messy because you are messy. Any day now the world's human population will reach eight billion. We each have our own mess, and of course, if you add all those little messes together it becomes significant. This isn't necessarily good or bad. It isn't necessarily a problem. The problem occurs when we try to live as if it isn't so.

Paul the apostle observed, "The good that I would, I do not; and the evil that I would not, I do." What was he saying? We don't do what we say we will do. We don't do what we intend to do. We often don't even do the things we most want to do. And worse than that, we often do things we know are bad for us, things we know will hurt other people, things that we know we will regret. And we do all these things even though deep down we don't want to do them.

Life should be lived with maximum intentionality. But too often we are conflicted and confused. When we act in these states, we usually cause pain and suffering to ourselves and others. Clarity is necessary to live with great intentionality. But finding that clarity is almost impossible in the midst of this crazy, noisy, busy world. That's why having time in silence and solitude each day is essential.

Why is life messy? Life's messy because we are messy. But this is not the only reason. Life is messy for reasons that make sense, but it can also be messy in ways that can only be rightly defined as a mystery.

Life is also messy because it can be random and unpredictable. We don't like random and unpredictable. The illusion of control is one of the most powerful. The reality is that while we can influence a great many outcomes, we are not in control. Despite this indisputable reality, we waste so much energy laboring under the illusion, trying to control people, situations, and outcomes.

Life is messy, but it isn't just a mess. Life is also wonderful. But this is the perspective that departs us when we are in the thick of the mess. We lose sight of all the good and get consumed by the turmoil we are embroiled in. We are tempted at these times to think that life will never be good again. This is the perspective that steals away our hope. The whole truth is that life is messy, but it is also wonderful and beautiful and awe-inspiring.

When I began scribbling in this notebook, I had lost this more complete perspective and was trying desperately to recover it. I knew I was lost and that was a grace. But that was all I knew in those dark moments. I didn't know how to get unlost. So, I would write, in hopes that, consciously or unconsciously, I would scribble something down that would point the way toward a brighter future. Wherever you are in your life, I hope these words do the same for you.

Life is messy because we are messy. The way forward always requires that we take responsibility for our part in the mess.

Have that conversation.

There is a conversation that you need to have. You know it. You may be avoiding it. Whatever conversation you are most afraid to have is probably the conversation you need most right now.

When evil comes to visit.

It was during this time in my life that evil came to visit. I had witnessed evil and brushed up against it many times before then. But in those days, it came to visit, pulled up a chair in the middle of my living room, and made its presence known and felt, day after day, for weeks and months.

It is popular these days to dismiss the idea of good and evil as the nonsense of another age. But evil exists. When forced to acknowledge the devastating reality of evil, our tendency is to think of it as something far away. Until one day you turn the corner and there it is, and your life will never be the same.

The sad and tragic truth is that evil is never far away. Not far from where you sit right now, men, women, and children, are being forced into every type of slavery and prostitution, by people so feral they are more like wild beasts than like people. Not far from where you sit right now, domestic violence and child abuse in all their forms are raging. Not far from where you sit right now, someone just bought a gun to kill himself or others. Not far from where you sit right now, drugs are being sold to children and changing the direction of their lives forever. Not far from where you sit right now, someone is being tortured, taken advantage of, blackmailed, corrupted, intimidated. Not far from where you sit at this moment, there are too many people who have nothing to lose. Not far from where you sit right now, children are so hungry they cannot sleep.

Evil is never far away. It is real and it is near.

I have witnessed evil. But witnessing evil in the lives of others is not the same as being touched by evil yourself. The touch of evil is something you never forget. It chills you to the bone, and leaves you in a white-hot rage.

When evil comes into your life, it becomes a presence. For a long time, it stands in the middle of every room demanding our attention. It is impossible to look away. As time passes, it can be moved into the corner of the room, then into the next room, and then into the basement or backyard. But once your life has been touched by evil, that presence never leaves you. There will be good days and bad days, and the bad days come out of nowhere, when you least expect them, and you don't know why.

It was during this time in my life that evil haunted me day and night. I survived, but at a cost. And those experiences will hang over me the rest of my life. They wounded me in ways I never imagined possible. I will never be the same. Everything I do and say for the rest of my life will be informed by those experiences. And so will everything I write. But I live in the hope that those torments will make me a better man.

Life can change in a single moment.

Life can change in a single moment. This is not just the stuff of movies and fairy tales. Your life really can change in an instant, for better or for worse.

I remember sitting at breakfast in New York City, at the Athletics Club overlooking Central Park, the day I made my first publishing deal. John F. Kennedy Jr. was sitting at the next table. I can still taste the fresh cut slices of pineapple. Later that morning I walked into a publishing meeting that changed my life forever. A few short years later, I watched the news that John F. Kennedy Jr.'s plane had gone down off Martha's Vineyard. A single tragic accident had ended his life.

Some life-changing moments lift up our hearts and make us feel like we are on top of the world, but others are soul-crushing. I was experiencing the soul-crushing variety.

Life can change in the blink of an eye, but most of the significant changes in our lives build over time before compounding into something wonderful or devastating. Anyone who has loved an addict or narcissist knows this all too well. As does anyone who has worked their whole life to develop a talent only to be discovered in an unexpected place at an unexpected time.

I have had more than my fair share of everything good that life has to offer. But it's the unexpected nature of the worst experiences of our lives that exacerbates the way they devastate us. Something happens and because of it everything changes. You will never be the same, your life will never be the same, your heart will never be the same, but life presses on with or without you, relentlessly pushing you toward the unknown future.

Three times before I was forty, I sat in a doctor office and was told I had cancer. Three unrelated cases. The first time I was thirty-five. I remember leaving the doctor's office in a daze, my life had just changed in an instant. I was face to face with my mortality for the first time. I sat in my car for about twenty minutes before I even started it, and I have vivid memories of the whole world swirling around me. What seemed important an hour ago no longer mattered. People rushing here and there, going about their lives, oblivious to the fact that the whole direction of my life had just shifted. It's a lonely feeling. The second time I was thirty-eight and the third time was the following year. The third encounter led to the removal of a large portion of my right kidney.

But nobody gave me cancer. It just happened. It was just part of life. There was nobody to blame, no one to harbor anger and resentment toward. That makes it easier.

It's when a person intentionally hurts you, changes your life in an instant, that you face the darkest parts of yourself. It's when a group of people decide to harm you, collectively or one at a time, that your faith in humanity is tested.

Slow down.

This was the next thing I wrote in my journal, "You are way over the speed limit of life. You need to slow down."

Life isn't a race. This is one of those quintessential lessons that we all hear at different times in our lives. We say to ourselves, "Got it." But we don't. Enjoy the journey. Another one of those lessons. We tell ourselves, "Got it." But we don't. We continue to rush around like maniacs.

But here's the real problem with racing through life. If you think of life as a race, every step sidewards and backwards, every pause, will seem like it doesn't belong, like a waste of time.

Every step is part of life, and there is life in every step. Life isn't a race, it's a dance. Every step forward and every step back, stepping sidewards and twirling in circles, are all part of the dance we call life.

Great dancers are never in a hurry. They relax into the rhythm, become one with their partners, and experience the exhilaration of the dance. When was the last time your life felt like that?

Simply slowing down improves almost everything in our lives.

The normalization of evil.

What is evil? Evil is defined as profoundly immoral. The definition itself holds the reason for the escalating evil in our world, though it may not be obvious at first. It all hinges on the word *immoral*.

The word *immoral* presents an intricate problem for our culture. Morality is almost never mentioned. I cannot recall the last time I heard the mainstream media describe something as immoral. Every type of perversion and depravity has become someone's personal preference and right.

When we pretend that there is no such thing as right and wrong, good and bad, this will inevitably lead to the proliferation of evil. And it has.

When immorality becomes your morality, you are profoundly lost. And immorality has become the morality of an alarming number of the most influential people in our society.

Our daily consumption of media and entertainment that relentlessly celebrate immorality as personal preference, and depravity as a personal right, has desensitized us to the reality and effects of evil.

The normalization of every immoral act on television continuously interferes with our moral compass. We can no longer discern true north. How is this normalization of staggeringly grotesque and immoral acts accomplished? Gradually and by repetition.

Track the history of depicting violence, drug use, murder, nudity, and graphic sexual assault in entertainment—with these two themes in mind—and it is easy to see how we ended up here. It happened gradually and with relentless repetition. It is the story of the frog in boiling water. We are the frog.

This is how we become desensitized to evil. It should be no surprise that we now have generations of morally ambivalent people living value-free lives. This is how every form of evil is permitted to thrive in society: poverty, oppression, destruction, violence, discrimination, corruption and slavery, to name but a few.

The evil you normalize will occur ever increasingly in society.

Every age has new storytellers, but one truth endures: We become the stories we read, hear, and watch. Today's storytellers appear to be committed to the normalization of evil, and by extension the annihilation of human dignity. Not the dignity of some anonymous people, but the annihilation of your dignity, my dignity, and the dignity of our spouses, children, grandchildren, friends, colleagues, and neighbors. Evil is much closer than we suspect.

Dehumanization.

What's really happening here? We are dehumanizing a whole civilization by desensitizing people to evil. When you dehumanize people, *it changes the way they treat each other*. People begin to debase each other, rather than ennobling each other. For example, brutality debases us, while love and respect ennoble us. Do we live in a society of love and respect or a society of brutality? The question itself is unsettling. The answer is not binary, but still, too much of our society is engaged in various forms of brutality to dismiss the question.

We sterilize every form of brutality by placing it at a distance and depersonalizing it. We prefer hypothetical and philosophical discussions about evil to personal exploration of the topic. But the effects of evil are always deeply personal.

Rape is one of the most brutal acts a person can experience, and one of the most dehumanizing, and it has been increasingly depicted on television.

One in six women in America has been a victim of rape. This is just one statistic. There are dozens that could be cited, one more disturbing than the last. But statistics are cold and distant. They allow us to place evil at a distance. So let me say it another way. One in six of our daughters, wives, sisters, and mothers have been raped.

It is also worth noting that the rape of a male is virtually nonexistent on television, making this particular form of brutality and dehumanization almost exclusively aimed at women in entertainment. The word itself should give us pause: *entertainment*. Rape as a form of entertainment. Isn't that what we are talking about in the context of television, movies, and books? Annihilating the dignity of women in this way goes virtually unchallenged.

This is just one example. Evil is real and much closer than we want to acknowledge. But I have never heard of anyone winning a war by pretending they weren't on the battlefield. Until evil touches us in an inescapably personal way, we either don't think of it at all or we think of it as something distant.

Closer than you think.

If we really want to understand the mess, we have to explore our role in it. The uncomfortable reality is that we all participate in evil. We avoid acknowledging this by confining our conversations about evil to things that we think we would never do or by avoiding the conversation altogether. But it's true, we all participate in evil.

Let's consider the definition of evil again. Evil is defined as profoundly immoral. Have you ever done something that has negatively altered the course of your life or someone else's? That's profoundly immoral.

I've done it. I did it yesterday. It will take great effort not to do it again today. Most of us participate in evil every day and are oblivious to it. The most common and insidious example is gossip. It is perhaps the everyday evil that has been most normalized.

If you were planning to murder someone, I suspect you would have all types of anxious feelings leading up to the event. But if you murdered someone every day, how long would it be before you no longer had those feelings? Human beings can become desensitized to even the most horrific things, and we have become desensitized to how profoundly gossip affects everyone involved. Most of us don't think of ourselves as murderers, but it is so easy to murder someone's reputation with gossip.

The power of speech is unfathomable. Gossip can never be undone. It is cruel, divisive, and demeaning. It alters the way people see another person forever. It robs the victim of dignity and opportunity.

I am ashamed that I have engaged in gossip about others.

Even as I write these words, I observe myself sterilizing the act, distancing myself from it with my choice of words: *engaged*. But I know I have harmed people by participating in this everyday evil. They may never know the harm I have caused them, but that doesn't make it less so. I know I caused harm to their reputations, and it is impossible for me to know the pain that I caused them or the opportunities they were excluded from because of my gossip. I have also been the coward who sat silently and listened passively, while others assassinated someone's character. And I have been the fool who piled on when others were gossiping about a person, kicking a man while he was down.

We have all been on the other side of this injustice too. You have suffered at the hands of gossips. I have too. I have been murdered a thousand times by gossip. It's an occupational hazard for anyone whose work puts them under public scrutiny, but that doesn't make it easier.

This is why I chose gossip as our example of everyday evil, because I don't know a single person who hasn't been the perpetrator and the victim. We have all been on both sides of this evil.

Gossip can destroy a person's reputation, affect the direction of their lives forever, and shatter their self-esteem. It can also lead to anxiety, depression, addiction, suicidal thoughts, and so many other outcomes that cannot be foreseen. The unintended consequences of gossip are of a different magnitude than the intended consequences. The intended consequences may be micro, while the unintended consequences are macro. Gossip can literally ruin a person's life.

Let's look now at the harm gossip causes us. Gossip hardens our hearts. You have to harden your heart toward a person in order to gossip about him or her. This hardening of the heart is an unavoidable prerequisite of gossip. But when we harden our hearts toward one person, we harden our hearts toward all people, including ourselves. Gossip therefore leads us to become indifferent to another person's suffering. This is just one way it dehumanizes us.

Gossip attacks our own self-esteem. Pointing out the faults and imperfections of others only draws attention to our own faults and imperfections. How do you feel when you gossip? You were probably disgusted with yourself in the moment. Did you think more of yourself or less of yourself after gossiping? How do you think it made the person you were gossiping with feel about you? If you do something that causes you to think less of yourself, isn't it inevitable that others will also think less of you?

Gossip is a destroyer of relationships. It breeds distrust and bitterness. People don't like people who gossip, and they don't trust them. Gossip promotes envy and division, and it will ultimately separate us from people. When we gossip, we are announcing to the world that we speak maliciously about others, that we are insecure or feel threatened, and that we cannot be trusted. Gossip divides and destroys.

Gossip plays havoc with our emotions. It breeds fear,

anger, jealousy, paranoia, anxiety, depression, and even hatred. It also leads to loneliness, because knowing that we cannot be trusted leads us to think that others cannot be trusted and that we are all alone in this world. The toxicity of gossip makes our souls sad. And if there is one thing we should pay very close attention to, it's anything that makes us soul-sad.

Every day we participate in conversations that could easily turn into gossip if we are not careful. How do we know when a conversation crosses that line? We could put together a list that includes speaking negatively or maliciously about someone, making a person appear incompetent or adequate, making public what should be kept private, criticizing or lying about a person, and so on. It would be a long list. But gossip is one of those things, you know it when you see it.

It doesn't hurt to have a couple of quick litmus tests at the ready to gain clarity as situations are playing out. Will other people think less of the person you are speaking about if you say what you are about to say? Would you like someone else to say those things about you? Reason and motive are also powerful indicators. Why are you saying it? Do you have a valid reason for saying what you are saying? What is your motive for saying it?

When you find yourself on the receiving end of evil you feel ludicrously impotent—because you are. Try to gather up one piece of gossip, just one lie that has been told about you, and you quickly discover how impossible it is to erase gossip from people's hearts and minds. That's the thing about evil, it makes you feel helpless, powerless, impotent.

If I had a dollar for every time...

This phrase originates from the writings of Mark Twain. In his book *More Tramps Abroad*, he wrote, "If I had a dollar for every person killed by snakebite per year in India I would rather have it than any other property." It has been used in many forms since, though perhaps never again in relation to snakebites. The dollar has been replaced with a nickel, penny or quarter. The snakebite has been replaced with too many things to mention. But the point is, most people realize that if they could receive a small sum for something that happens often, they could become wealthy. In Mark Twain's case that was snakebites and fifty-thousand people die of snakebite each year in India—a number that has remained astoundingly steady since he penned those words.

Now imagine you had a dollar for every time someone gossiped about someone else. This business is called social media. Today the most valuable platform is worth more than $850 billion.

Some people will defend social media, citing its virtues, such as: staying connected with family and friends, online learning, opportunities for remote work, quick access to information, and philanthropic and civic engagement. But its vices are considerable: narcissistic behavior; cyberbullying; social media addiction; self-esteem issues; impatience;

shortened attention span; social anxiety; fake friends; sexual predation; unrealistic perception of other people's lives; unrealistic expectations of one's own life; confusion about the nature of friendship; hyperbolic peer pressure; invasion of privacy; identity theft; behavior monitoring; toxic, offensive, demeaning, and inappropriate content; mental health issues; sleep deprivation; the dominance of extremism over rational, measured voices; decreased creativity; censorship; and of course, the industrialization of gossip.

Social media has made it easier than ever to ruin a person's reputation. The damage you can do to a person via these platforms is almost limitless. This is especially true because the world of social media is uniquely unforgiving. Do you want to live in a world without forgiveness? A world without second chances and new beginnings? Do you want to live in a world where you don't even get a chance to admit that you were wrong and that you can do better? A world where you are just written off and dismissed? This is the world social media has created.

There are also other significant and far-reaching problems that have emerged from this industrialization of gossip—two in particular.

First, social media has shifted the burden of proof from the accuser to the accused. Guilt by accusation is very dangerous indeed. There are significant reasons the legal systems in all *civilized* nations place the burden of proof on the accuser. Primary among them is the fact that it is impossible in most situations to prove innocence. This is why our legal system considers a defendant innocent until proven guilty. It is also why a defendant is declared not guilty rather than innocent. By shifting the burden of proof, social media has become uniquely uncivilized.

The rise of social media has also caused irreparable damage to the craft of reporting the news. The skill, integrity, and professionalism required to accurately report the happenings of this world are quickly becoming a lost craft. Opinion now dominates news. The quest for truth has been subordinated to personal agendas. The media is no longer satisfied with the humble professionalism of reporting the actual news and letting us decide for ourselves what it means. Swept up in self-importance and celebrity, they now feel the need to tell us what to think about the news.

Would news broadcasting have shifted further and further in this direction if social media had not entered our culture? It is a question worthy of consideration.

There is no question that the quality and integrity of the news media was much higher before the rise of social media. The immense popularity of social media has dragged news further and further toward entertainment. In an effort to compete with social media, traditional news outlets have drenched themselves with opinion in a futile effort to hold onto people's attention, ratings, and advertisers. The craft of reporting the news has been replaced by a new entertainment art that prioritizes opinions and agendas over the facts of the stories being reported.

How will the news media reinvent itself next? Where is the new opportunity? My hope is that a growing percentage of people at both ends of the political spectrum would like to have the news reported to them accurately and without bias or opinion.

The quantity of news coverage is measurably greater than ever before, but the quality of the news being reported has been significantly compromised. This is the question I find myself pondering: Which of the most important stories reported over the past fifty years would not be reported in today's environment?

The negative impact of social media is only beginning to be discovered, but you can be sure it is more far-reaching than the self-esteem of teenagers. The way it is being used to attack our rule of law and destroy the way news is reported are just two examples. Social media is like a drug that has been on the market for twenty years before they discover it is causing cancer.

I appreciate that some people will argue that social media is responsible for some good in the world. I don't disagree. But if I murdered people every day and then volunteered at the local soup kitchen serving the homeless on Saturday mornings, at what point would you question my integrity?

Social media has industrialized and commercialized gossip. It is the most effective tool for negativity in the history of the world, profiting every day from the misery of millions. If gossip is dehumanizing, social media is the systematic dehumanization of a whole culture. If we reflect on our discussion about evil and gossip, at some point, all men and women of goodwill have questions to consider. Does social media advance or detract from a person's ultimate happiness? Is it possible the world would be better off without it?

More concerning than the answers to these questions is our unwillingness to rigorously explore the questions themselves as individuals and as a society. I am not fool enough to think that we can put social media back in Pandora's box, but exploring these questions can radically alter the role we allow it to play in our lives and in society. But perhaps the reason we refuse to do so is because we are afraid we will discover that the internet is a modern version of Pandora's box—a gift that at first seems valuable, but in reality is a curse, the source of great and unexpected troubles.

The great rehumanization.

The future of humanity depends on a great movement of rehumanization. This is a vast claim, but I believe it to be true and don't make it lightly.

What is rehumanization? Rehumanization is an effort to reverse the effects of dehumanization by restoring human dignity, helping each and every person develop a healthy sense of self, and reprioritizing people above money, objects, systems, and institutions.

Rehumanization is about learning to be human again,

which may sound strange, but it's amazing how often and in how many ways the average person experiences dehumanization.

Dehumanization takes many forms. Some things are dehumanizing by their very nature, for example, violence, slavery, abuse, injustice, torture, poverty, sexual abuse, discrimination, gossip, objectification and genocide. There are many other things that can be dehumanizing, such as: work, technology, debt, humor, laws, entertainment, social media, and even education or consensual sex.

Anytime the value and individuality of a person are being denied, that person is being dehumanized. And the more someone has been dehumanized, the more that person will operate out of the primal tendencies of fight-or-flight.

The process of rehumanization reminds us what it means to be an individual of worth. It rekindles a healthy sense of personal identity and helps us rediscover our humanity.

Rehumanization is about learning to see ourselves and others as human again. It may sound ridiculous, but you would be amazed at how many ways we have been conditioned not to see ourselves as human beings. One of the most blatant and common examples is our inability to express our needs. To be human is to need, and yet, we have been conditioned to believe that it is not alright to need certain things.

In order to see and value the humanity of another person we have to be able to see and value our own humanity. Learning to accept that we are wounded and broken is essential to the process of rehumanization. Discovering your own brokenness and realizing that you can be put back together and healed to become more beautiful and more lovable than ever before is the summit of rehumanization.

Human beings with a healthy sense of self, when their basic needs are met and their survival is not threatened, want good things for other people. Anyone who wishes another person unhappiness or harm, anyone who doesn't desire good for others, is in a dehumanized condition. Emotionally healthy human beings desire good for each other. At our best, we are kind, well-meaning, generous, compassionate, benevolent, thoughtful, sensitive, tender, warmhearted, and empathic.

Empathy is a leading indicator of human flourishing, while lack of empathy is a signal that a person is in a dehumanized state. Empathy is the natural condition for a human being who is mentally, emotionally, and spiritually healthy. This is what it means to be humane.

It is time to turn our efforts toward the great rehumanization of the human family. It's time to focus on things that support humanization. It's time to celebrate those things that bring out the best in people.

To accomplish this, a great shift in our culture is necessary. Our focus on money dehumanizes our relationships by making them transactional. Our focus on things leads us to dehumanize each other by objectifying people. Our focus on appearances dehumanizes our relationships by making them disingenuous. It's time to move beyond a money-oriented way of life, beyond an object-oriented way of life, beyond an appearance-oriented lifestyle, and create a people-oriented society.

Is there any more urgent task before society today? Which of our problems would not be solved by seeing ourselves and others as human beings again, and treating ourselves and others as human beings of infinite individual value? Let's put our efforts toward rehumanization.

While we are wasting endless hours on social media or whatever our preferred way of wasting time is, the great suffering in the world goes unaddressed. I think about my own collaboration with evil. I think about the many times I have hurt other people throughout my life—sometimes intentionally, but mostly out of self-absorption and lack of awareness. I think about the ways I have dehumanized others. Two things haunt me when I reflect on these things: the hurt I have caused and the good I could have been doing if I hadn't been so busy being stupid and selfish.

The subtlest evil of all is the opposite of love. It is diabolical and insidious. It isn't hatred, there is nothing subtle about hatred. The opposite of love is indifference. It is the Pied Piper that leads millions into despair. But indifference is not a force unto itself in this universe. It can only be expressed by one person to another person, from one group of people to another group of people. Indifference cannot survive in this world outside the human heart. So let us banish it from our hearts.

We have all been indifferent toward the dehumanization of other people, perhaps because we have been dehumanized ourselves. Now is the time to embrace our own rehumanization and champion the rehumanization of every man, woman, and child.

Ambassadors of hope.

There is a battle raging in each and every human heart. This battle is between hope and despair and we can tip the balance by embracing the call to become ambassadors of hope.

Many years ago, I was on my way home from work and a friend came to mind. It occurred to me that I hadn't heard from him for a few days, and I knew he had been having a tough time. I have no idea what led me to do so, but I drove to his place on the other side of town to visit him.

When he opened the door, he looked horrible. The place was dark and there was trash everywhere. We opened the curtains to let some light in, and a few windows to get some fresh air circulating. I suggested he shave and take a shower, while I ordered a pizza and tidied up a bit. He resisted for a moment, but I said, "Come on, you'll feel so much better, and when you're done the pizza will be here." We sat on his front porch eating pizza and telling stories, and when we were done, I drove home.

The next day I opened my mailbox to find this handwritten note from him: *"I was going to kill myself last night, but then you stopped by just to say hello, and I thought to myself somebody does care. So, thank you."*

Something like that stops you in your tracks. It reminds you how powerful our actions are and how tragic inaction can be. I knew he had been having a tough time, but I never imagined he would do something so drastic.

Today that man is a doctor. He has a wife and three children, a mortgage and a dog. On that night all those years ago, he was just going through a rough patch. We have never spoken of that evening all those years ago, but he knows, and I know. What do we know? We know that we can call each other at any hour of the day or night, and that we will be there for each other, whatever the need may be.

The point is our actions can tip the balance between hope and despair. That is a power that should be used often and respected always.

Thoughtless, careless, and reckless.

We have all seen people behave recklessly and carelessly. Perhaps we wonder to ourselves: How could someone behave so recklessly?

The origin of recklessness is thoughtlessness. We have all been thoughtless, and we have all been the victims of other people's thoughtlessness. It stings but the pain doesn't linger for long. If we are thoughtless often enough, we become careless. If you have ever been on the receiving end of carelessness, you know it changes you. When people are careless with our safety, or careless with our trust, or careless with our hearts, it hurts. This pain is real.

Depending on how egregious the carelessness is we may never fully recover. It has the potential to make us cynical, jaded, untrusting, and miserable. But it changes most people in this way: We become more cautious with people, we are gentler with others, and we give them the benefit of the doubt, because we don't want to be on the giving end of carelessness.

This is how suffering at the hands of other people's carelessness affected me. It caused me to slow down. It made me dread being careless myself and inflicting the same anguish on someone else.

Like all bad traits, carelessness is dehumanizing. It dehumanizes the person being careless and the person they are careless toward. What part of our humanity is eroded? Tenderness. Carelessness robs us of our tenderness. People who are careless on a regular basis become incapable of tenderness toward others. People who have been victimized by carelessness withhold their tenderness in an effort to stay safe.

Thoughtlessness leads to carelessness, and carelessness sets the stage for recklessness. Beware reckless people: they will destroy you on the way to destroying themselves. A person who is reckless, or in a reckless state, has no regard for other people's safety, comfort, or needs. She is oblivious to the dangers of a situation and indifferent to the consequences of her actions. He will lie about things for no reason and not care even when he knows he is being hurtful. She will refuse to apologize for anything, or apologize and not mean it. He lacks all empathy. She refuses to control her impulses. He enjoys manipulating others. She will get angry for no reason. He is completely self-centered. A reckless person may see fear, sadness, or disappointment in your eyes, but will carry on regardless. It's impossible to justify recklessness, but they will try, and in the process make you wonder if you are crazy. Reckless people are very dangerous indeed. Recklessness ruins lives.

During these three years of my life, I was on the receiving end of more thoughtlessness, carelessness, and recklessness than the rest of my life entire. Like waves crashing on the beach, it seemed relentless. One situation would knock me down and I would pull myself to my feet, only to be demolished by another wave of carelessness or recklessness.

Do they know how much suffering they caused me? That's a depressing road to go down. There are days I wish I could wallow in self-pity, but there are three things that always drag me out of that pit and give me some unwanted perspective. Those three things are my own thoughtlessness, carelessness, and recklessness.

There is a harsh truth to face. I have been all these things. Sometimes I stare off into space thinking about the people I have hurt. I wish I could go back and do things differently, but I can't. I wish I could do something now to make up for my selfishness then, but in most cases I cannot. It makes me sad, but that sadness makes me a better husband and father, a better son, brother, and friend. A better human being. It increases my awareness and makes me evermore thoughtful of how my words and actions affect others. And there is another harsh truth to face. I still have a long way to go, because I still find myself slipping into thoughtlessness.

Mercy.

We used to play a game called *Mercy* at school when I was child. Two players grasp each other's hands and interlock their fingers. Each player attempts to bend back his opponent's hand or twist their fingers until the opponent surrenders by crying out "Mercy!"

Sometimes I wish I could call mercy on life, and that doing so would relieve the pressure and the pain, not indefinitely, just long enough for me to catch my breath and recollect myself.

Future turmoil.

There will be more turmoil in my future. I know that. Life is messy and it stays messy. What I have shared with you in these pages are my reflections based on an incredibly difficult time in my life. I survived. Those days are far enough behind me now to reflect upon them with clear eyes. There are still days when I look back and sadness overwhelms me, and days I choose not to look back. Will it always be so? I don't know.

The future is uncertain but not completely unknown.

There will be more storms in my life and yours. I know that. I just don't know when. There will be more turmoil ahead. I am sure of that, though I know not what disguise it will come wearing.

More people will lie to me, try to use and manipulate me for their own purposes, and more betrayal is never out of the question. Still, I refuse to lose faith in people. I refuse to lose sight of all the good. I have come to the realization that most of the suffering people cause, most of the atrocities they commit, are unconscious. "They know not what they do," was Jesus' assessment and I have witnessed this truth over and again. And yet, human beings are gloriously capable of love and kindness, and every manner of goodness. And it seems that when their survival is not threatened, if they have not been dehumanized, they much prefer goodness over all else.

Life is difficult.

Life is difficult. We can accept that or get aggravated, but we cannot change it. The mistake we make, with varying degrees of awareness, is that we believe life should be easy, and that we would be happier if it were. We torture ourselves when we conflate easy with good and difficult with bad. This false belief leads to a clash of the titans between reality and our illusions.

The easy life is a mirage. Those who chase this illusion end up angry, broken, disappointed, cynical, and resentful. Anyone who thinks life should be easy will lack empathy for others in their struggles. They will also lack empathy for themselves when they are being tossed about by life's difficulties. In the extreme, when their own life gets difficult, they may come to believe there is something wrong with themselves.

The problem isn't that life is difficult. It is supposed to be difficult. The problem is that we expect it to be easy or we try to make it easy. Life proposes a series of challenges, dilemmas, problems, dissatisfactions, heartaches, and opportunities. How we respond to these events determines the direction and quality of our lives. But we have become so expert at problem-solving, that we think that life itself is a problem to solve. But the "life-is-difficult problem" is unsolvable because it isn't a problem.

We set out to avoid all difficulty and friction. This is impossible, so we become agitated and angry. We shun anything that will bring us stress. Pain is unacceptable in this paradigm, so each time we encounter it we try to numb it.

All our efforts to avoid the difficulties of life lead us away from everything that is deeply satisfying. If your goal was an easy life, would any of the following be possible? Meaningful relationships, deeply satisfying work, health and vitality, raising children, starting a business, or mastery of a profession or hobby?

What are you avoiding that you should be confronting?

This quest for the easy life leads us into the abyss of comfort. We begin to see comfort as the antidote for anything that is difficult. But soon the comfort turns to pain. I know, it's a paradox, but it is real. It may not be physical pain, but emotional pain and spiritual angst. We are not made for an easy life, so with each attempt at the easy life we inflict acute emotional suffering upon ourselves.

We now find ourselves at a junction. We can return to reality and face head-on the difficulties of life, or we can allow reality to continue to crash against our illusion of an easy life. Many choose their illusions, but they end up suffering more for their avoidance than they would have suffered if they had simply embraced the difficulties of life. Having abandoned the path that leads to everything deeply satisfying, they become miserably discontented, and spend their lives complaining about everything and everyone. Only a fool makes an easy life his ultimate goal.

When human beings are at their best, they face the difficulties of life head-on. They learn to delay gratification, embrace reality, release illusions, accept responsibility for their lives, and live in the wisdom that the most satisfying experiences are often difficult.

Turning to comfort.

It is natural to turn to comfort during times of pain, distress, exhaustion, trauma, and suffering. Comfort has a role to play in our lives, but few things will test our wisdom and virtue more than discerning a right relationship with comfort.

Before these dark times, I had never asked an elementary question: What is the purpose of comfort? It's fascinating how something as commonplace as comfort can go unquestioned for so long.

The purpose of comfort is healing, rejuvenation, and renewal. It serves us by providing relief from pain and suffering, easing distress, and helping us transcend experiences. It prepares us to face the challenges and opportunities of life again.

But there is also a dark side to comfort. It is seductive and can easily become a way of life. When comfort becomes the goal of our lives, we begin a debilitating downward spiral. Once we are addicted to comfort, it shifts from strengthening us to weakening us.

Comfort is a beautiful servant, but an ugly master. It is a cunning and wicked tyrant. Little by little, it syphons off your soul strength, and you find yourself incapable of facing your daily responsibilities. With your soul strength sapped, you become morally, ethically, and spiritually paralyzed. This paralysis prevents you from standing up for what is good, right, true, and just. At this point you are living for comfort. All you want now is comfort, but no comfort is enough to satisfy you.

If you want to destroy people, make them comfortable. Give them every comfort they desire. Excessive indulgence in comfort always leads to love of comfort, and love of comfort poisons the soul. How? Comfort reduces our ability to hear truth and align our lives with it.

When we hear truth, we have one of two reactions. If we are living the truth we hear, we delight in the splendor of it. If we are not living that truth, we become uncomfortable, because unlived truth is always an invitation to adjust our lives to align with the truth being revealed. Truth can be very uncomfortable, so a lover of comfort closes himself off from it, even the truth that would liberate him from his addiction to comfort.

Comfort also reduces our ability to have difficult conversations with people. It numbs our sense of justice by overwhelming it with self-interest. It gives us a false sense of security, while creating an insatiable dependency. It smothers our curiosity and creativity, and robs us of our very sense of self.

How many people in our culture are addicted to comfort? Perhaps we are all addicted to comfort to varying degrees. We each disguise our illicit relationship with comfort in our own ways. I have an unhealthy relationship with it. It seems I am constantly struggling to find the right balance. I just pray I will continue to struggle to find the life-giving place for comfort in my life.

Just as life is not meant to be easy, it is not supposed to be comfortable. Be ever vigilant of the role you allow comfort to play in your life. Allow it to serve you in your trials and tribulations, and at the end of a long day of exertion, but do not become a lover of comfort. Comfort will destroy you long before the difficulties of life.

Inspiration.

There are some comforts that will never poison your soul. Inspiration is first among them. The word literally means, *to breathe life into.* If you must seek comfort, seek those which raise you up.

Inspiration brings the best out of us. Inspiration plays a critical role in our lives. It can be the difference between feeling fully alive and the drudgery of slogging your way through another day.

What inspires you? Books? Movies? Comedy? Music? Nature? Prayer? People? Whatever it is, find a way to build it into your daily routine.

We thrive if we have a steady stream of inspiration. Many of us have never experienced that. We get a little bit here and there, from time to time, but a steady stream of inspiration is life changing.

Inspiration stimulates our creativity, and creativity affects everything. When we are in a creative space, we listen differently, love differently, work differently, spend money differently, parent differently, and make decisions on a higher level. We are altogether different when our creativity is firing. You see it in conversation all the time. I was talking with a friend the other day and asking him about a variety of topics. When the topic that inspired him came up, his posture changed, his face became animated, and his voice filled with enthusiasm.

We are at our best when we are inspired! Inspiration triggers creativity, and creativity changes the way we see everything and do anything.

You may be thinking that you are not a creative person. You may have been told this at some time in your life, but it isn't true. The idea that some people are creative and other people aren't is a myth.

We are all creative. Creativity is a human quality that we all possess. You may not be able to paint like Michelangelo. That's okay. If creativity expressed itself the same way in everyone that would be boring. It manifests differently from one person to the next. Creativity has an infinite number of expressions.

Anytime someone does something with passion and purpose, even the most ordinary things, you are witnessing creativity. Yes, we see this passion and purpose in musicians and artists, but we also see it in nurses and teachers, firefighters and entrepreneurs, mothers and fathers.

Creativity is everywhere if you know how to look for it. And it is in you. Learn how to feed yourself a steady diet of inspiration and you will live and love more creatively.

Cherish the ordinary.

It was the ordinary things that saved me. I have experienced enough extraordinary to know that I would choose the ordinary over the extraordinary all day long. Learn to cherish the ordinary. Make a list of twenty ordinary things that bring you joy when you experience them consciously.

Here's my list: Breathing. Sleeping. Waking. Water. Nature. Food. Reading. Thinking. Conversation. Music. Art. Seasons. Friendship. Children. Kindness. Chocolate. Laughter. Hugs. Holding hands. Home.

Allow the ordinary to heal you.

Just for the joy of it.

"How do you know if you're a good father?" my friend asked me as we sat on the park bench. Our small children were playing on a playset and the soccer field before us. "You're a good father!" I replied.

"You say that," he persisted, "but that isn't an answer to the question. How do you know I'm a good father?" He was right. I hadn't answered the question, and it's an important one.

"I know you are a good father by the way your children play with other children. They don't just want to play; they want to play with others. If you brought them here alone, they would be ready to go home after fifteen minutes. But we will sit here for two hours and when we say it's time to go home, they will beg us for a few more minutes. They delight in playing with others. And I see your kids, they don't just want to have fun themselves. It's important to them that everyone else is having fun. They delight not only in their own happiness, but in the happiness of others."

He didn't say anything. We just sat there quietly watching our children play. And I started to think to myself, I need to learn how to play again.

So much of what we do, we do out of obligation – real or imagined. So much of what we do, we do because we think we have to. We do so many things in our quest to be efficient. But I sit here watching my children at play in the yard, and almost everything they do, they do simply for the joy of it.

What do you do just for the joy of it? When was the last

time you did something just for the joy of it? It is one of the things I admire in people. Many of the people I admire do much of what they do just for the joy of it. There are things they do because they are obligated to, and things they do because they promised they would, and there are things they do simply because they are the right things to do. But they have more of these other things in their lives, more of the things they do just for the joy of it.

If you look a little closer, you will discover something fascinating. For the most part, they do the same things that everyone else does, but they approach them very differently. They may work as hard as the next person, but they don't do it just to make money or because they have to, they have found a way to work joyfully. They don't focus on getting it finished so they can do something else. They focus on enjoying what they are doing and doing it well.

What can you do today just for the joy of it?

Everyone is fighting a hard battle.

My own struggle led me to become intimately aware that everyone is fighting a hard battle, carrying a heavy burden, and in some way just living from day to day. For hundreds of millions of people, the world is a brutal, sad, unjust, and maddening place. Are my woes less than theirs? I think they are. And still, I know it is unhealthy to try to explain away our own suffering. There is a way to acknowledge the great suffering of others without diminishing our own suffering.

Life is difficult. Not for some people, but for everyone in their own way. People don't walk around with a sign around their neck that announces what they are struggling with.

"I'm depressed."

"Yesterday I had a miscarriage."

"I lost my job two weeks ago, but I don't know how to tell my wife."

"My husband just told me he doesn't love me anymore."

"Am I a good mother?"

"I'm addicted to drugs."

"I want to break off my engagement."

"My son won't talk to me."

"I just found out I have cancer."

"I don't know what to do with my life."

People don't walk around with signs. But everyone's struggling with something. When we are mindful of this, we are gentler with others. When we forget this, we abandon our humanity.

Everyone you will ever meet is fighting a hard battle, even if it doesn't seem like it. We measure other people's lives by their blessings, but we don't see their hidden burdens. You never know what is going on inside somebody—and everyone has something going on inside them.

When we recognize that someone is fighting a hard battle, we tend to rise to the occasion. It brings out the best in us, and compassion and generosity begin to flow. So next time somebody is upsetting you, frustrating you, annoying you, or ignoring you, take a deep breath and remember that she is fighting her own hard battle. Allow the greatness of your humanity to rise up within you, and act with gentle compassion.

This was among the lessons I learned during this time of turmoil in my own life. It is a mistake to get completely absorbed in our own troubles. When we isolate ourselves, we don't cut ourselves off from the problems, we cut ourselves off from the solutions.

Beautiful Kindness.

It was people who ultimately drew me out of my sadness. It wasn't anything I wrote in my journal, it wasn't some great thought, and it wasn't something I did. It was people.

I wrote this in my journal, "She was so kind to me. I was hurt, so wounded, and suffering, and her kindness soothed me. She didn't even know she was doing it. Her kindness was as naturally a part of her as her eyes and hands were. Her beautiful kindness drew me out of my sadness."

But there were others too. Friends and family, perfect strangers, people I had known forever and people I had just met, each in their own way gifting me with a beautiful kindness.

One day I was lying on the couch in my study, in a daze, unable to move, held down by a debilitating sadness. Next thing I knew, my little boy Harry climbed up onto the couch and snuggled into me. I held him close, but perhaps he was holding me. The latter, I think. He didn't say a word. He didn't need to. Somehow, he knew that. Within ten or fifteen minutes, he had effortlessly lifted me out of that sadness. He knew that too. He kissed the side of my face, rolled off the couch, and disappeared as suddenly as he had arrived.

All the kindness was both random and yet coordinated. Each person was just doing what they felt called to do. Each act seemed random. But the Divine Physician was coordinating every kindness to heal my soul and restore my hope. It was a program of kindness God had designed just for me.

Came the day when I became conscious that in my desperate efforts to survive, I had neglected my own capacity for kindness. It is one of life's most delightful paradoxes: The more joy we bring to others, the more our own joy expands.

The greatness and beauty of the human spirit is undeniable in kindness. Kindness is beautiful, whether it is the thoughtfulness of a random act of kindness or the heroic kindness that involves great personal sacrifice. Examine the most devastating and disgusting moments in human history and you will find heroic kindness. The greatness of the human spirit often shines brightest when the world is darkest.

The Great Depression drew neighbors close together. They cared for each other, often going without so that their neighbor's children would have enough to eat. It is thoughtful kindness to share your food with others if you have plenty to eat yourself; it is heroic kindness to go hungry so another can eat.

World War II was one of the most horrific events in history. Eighty-five million people died. Fifty-seven million from activities directly related to the war, and another twenty-eight million died from war-related disease and famine. Still, in the midst of this intense evil, ordinary people were going without and risking their lives with their kindness. Thousands of people risked their own lives to hide Jews from the Nazis. In the process, they reminded these people who were being hunted like animals that all humanity had not been lost.

Viktor Frankl's experience of the culture within concentration camps provides significant insight. He noticed that there were some Nazi guards who showed kindness to prisoners, while there were some prisoners who would exploit their fellow prisoners for personal gain. Most significantly, he discovered that kindness helped people live longer. Prisoners who focused on themselves and fell into self-pity were significantly more likely to commit suicide or die of starvation even with equal rations.

Beyond the daily acts of kindness there were also heroic acts of kindness. One morning in Auschwitz, after a prisoner had escaped, the guards decided to murder ten prisoners to discourage others from trying to escape. One of the men selected cried out, "My wife! My children!" It was a desperate plea in the face of brutal inhumanity. The guards didn't care. But one of the man's fellow prisoners did. "I'll take his place," he announced. He stared directly into the face of Nazi brutality and provided an epic moment of kindness. In the face of cold indifference, it was a moment of glowing love. His name was Maximilian Kolbe.

We also see the enormity of the human heart whenever there is a natural disaster. Aid and relief pour in from around the world. Wherever there is suffering and pain, caused by evil or circumstances like natural disaster, there are always people doing their part, however small, to bring kindness to the situation. They refuse to let what they can't do interfere with what they can do.

In a world that can be cold, harsh, violent, and at times brutal, kindness proves that our humanity has a better side, a side that is caring and gentle, a side that can rise above almost anything.

Kindness is one of the utterly beautiful expressions of our humanity. Everyday kindness, random acts of kindness, and heroic moments of kindness banish fear, soothe pain, revive hope, and restore our faith in humanity. There are times in our lives when we desperately need to feel the touch of kindness. And there are times when what we need more than anything else is to extend this beautiful kindness to another.

The power of kindness is undeniable. It is one of your superpowers. Unleash it in your life and watch the domino effect of goodness that it sets off around you and within you. In the darkness, I discovered that even when we are paralyzed by pain, we are still capable of love, goodness, generosity, and the beautiful kindness that reminds us all what it means to be human.

Roses and people.

"When people show you who they are, believe them the first time," was Maya Angelou's observation. I agree, and I disagree. If someone does something horrific, you don't wait around for them to do it again. But there is a danger that we will be too quick to write people out of our lives.

I find it useful to distinguish between events and patterns. If somebody does something once, it's an event. If a person does the same thing twice or three times, it becomes a pattern. Learning to recognize patterns in people's behavior is essential in relationships, and not only other people's patterns, but our own. What are your patterns of behavior? Good and bad?

There are good and bad patterns in each life. It is important to be mindful of this. Compulsive behavior, impulsive behavior, addiction, and physical and emotional abuse are all negative patterns that can have disastrous effects. But there is also an endless array of positive patterns that enrich a person's life, and the lives of everyone close to them. Respect, continuous learning, exercise, a balanced diet, hard work, love, thoughtfulness, and appreciation are just a handful.

We reveal who we are with our actions. Don't let someone's apologies blind you to their actions, especially when their actions are clearly a pattern. Beware of patterns. When you see signs and red flags, don't ignore them. People are constantly telling you about who they are with their actions. It may be time to start listening more carefully.

There are three things I know about roses: They are beautiful. They all have thorns. I'd rather live in a world with roses than a world without roses. There are three things I know about people: They are beautiful. They all have thorns. I'd rather live in a world with people than a world without people.

Mourning the life that could have been.

In order to embrace the unexpected life, we need to mourn the life that could have been. Perhaps a dream didn't come true. Perhaps someone you loved died. Perhaps you were in an accident, deceived and manipulated by someone you trusted, or got your heart broken. Whatever the cause, the life you hoped and expected to live is gone now, and all that is left is the unexpected life.

Grieving is just one part of the healing process. The five stages of grieving are: denial, anger, bargaining, depression, and acceptance. It's a very neat and tidy process, isn't it? The reality of course is that life is messy, and we are intimately aware of that when we are grieving.

The process of grieving the life that could have been doesn't end. It diminishes over time and requires less emotional and psychological energy, but the smallest reminder of what you have lost can put you right back there again.

When we suffer trauma or loss, we are stunned and can become numb. After the initial shock wears off, we can experience stress, disorientation, anger, anxiety, and depression.

We can also fall into self-blame. We all adopt various coping mechanisms, some healthy and others unhealthy. We may think and say things like, "I just want to move on" or "I'm ready to put this whole thing behind me." But you can't just move on. You have to deal with it. Physical wounds get worse and can become life-threatening if you ignore them. Emotional wounds respond in exactly the same way. So do psychological and spiritual wounds. If you don't attend to your wound, it will begin to fester, causing discomfort at first, then pain, and will ultimately lead to the distortion of your personality.

And you can't just put the whole thing behind you. It's part of who you are now. You will absorb it into your life and process it in either a healthy or an unhealthy way. You may be able to control your emotions for a time, but grief affects the whole person: physically, emotionally, intellectually and spiritually.

Don't ignore the fact that you have been hurt. You may have been hurt by someone else, you may have hurt yourself. Whatever the case may be, acknowledge the pain and suffering that have been caused.

You may not want to appear vulnerable and weak. We should never want to appear to be anything other than what we are. When we make decisions based on how we want to appear to be, we make bad decisions.

When horrible things happen to us, we want to believe that there is a proper way to deal with the experience, to process it, to heal from it. Maybe there is and maybe there isn't. One thing is for sure and that is this: It is messy.

Mourn the life that could have been if your dream had come true, if your baby hadn't died, if you had not been betrayed, if your spouse had not divorced you, if you hadn't made such a devastating mistake, if you hadn't gotten sick. Mourn that life. It is a prerequisite for discovering the exquisite possibilities that still lay ahead.

The past.

During times of turmoil, we may feel like we are being pulled in two directions, into the past and toward the future.

Don't fear the past. You are not what has happened to you. You are not what you have accomplished. You are not even who you are today, or who you have become so far. You are also who and what you are still capable of becoming. You are your realized and unrealized potential. God sees you and all your potential, and he aches to see you embrace your best, truest, highest self. He yearns to help you and to accompany you in that quest.

Don't let your past define you. It may be helpful to glance in the rearview mirror from time to time, but if you keep your gaze there for too long you will crash.

Allow the past to serve you. Don't let it rob you of your now. Don't let it steal your future. Delve into it occasionally to learn more about yourself, but avoid lingering there for too long. If you sense you may be lingering in the past in an unhealthy way, ask yourself, how is this serving me?

Luck is a factor.

When I was younger, anytime luck was mentioned I had an aversion to it. I would say, "Luck is a self-inflicted state of mind." And I believed it. I think. I thought success in anything was the result of hard work, persistence, courage, and other things within my control. Life has taught me different.

Some events and outcomes in life, perhaps even most of them, can be attributed to internal influences like the choices we make and how hard we work. But there are other outcomes and events in life that can clearly be attributed to external influences, like a natural disaster or another person's choices. It's these external, unpredictable, unstable, uncontrollable forces that can deliver crushing blows.

We don't like to think of luck as a factor. It goes against our illusion of control.

What is luck? We use words and we assume we know what they mean, but we all define them in our own way. Luck is generally considered to be an outcome that is brought on by chance rather than one's own actions and efforts. But nothing is that clear or clean cut. Life is messy, as we have discovered. The false assumption here is that outcomes are the result of either one or the other. The reality is they are usually a combination of both. Even when another person makes a horrible choice and we suffer the consequences, very often we have chosen to have that person in our lives.

I worked hard on my craft when I was younger, but so do lots of other writers. When I was twenty-two years old, an author that I had never met, insisted that her agent come and hear me speak. After the event, I was introduced to an agent from one of the biggest literary agencies in the world. The William Morris Agency opened the doors to all the biggest publishers. They literally took me from one publisher to another introducing me and my work.

Was that luck? Fate? Destiny? Divine providence? The inevitable response to all my hard work? What role did my talent play? And what credit can I take for my success? Some but not all. Why did that author decide to do what she did? How would my life have been different if she hadn't? I don't know. I can't know. I will never know.

Luck is a factor, but how much is a mystery. There is such a thing as being in the right place at the right time, and the wrong place at the wrong time. And I do know that the harder you work the more luck and success you attract. Perhaps luck is one of those things that is dangerous to think too much about, but unwise to ignore altogether.

I have lived a fortunate life. Has life been easy? No. Have I suffered? Yes. Have I experienced good luck and bad luck? Yes. Is my fortunate life the result of my hard work alone? No.

Yes, I have worked hard. I have worked hard to improve my writing. I have worked hard to grow spiritually and develop character. I have diligently saved and invested some of the fruits of my work. I have dedicated myself to my primary relationships. I have worked hard to help others and make a contribution to society. I've worked hard but I have also been fortunate.

Sometimes when I say I have been lucky friends will say, "It's not luck. You have been blessed." I have been blessed, it's true, but I have also been lucky. The reason I cannot lay all my good fortune and success in the category of blessings is because to do so would be to accuse God of playing favorites. And I don't believe God has favorites.

If I had been born in the Sudan, I would have lived a very different life. If my parents were Chinese, I never would have been born. My mother would have been forced to have an abortion under their single child policy. I was born in a nation of liberty and rights. I was educated and given every chance to succeed in every aspect of life. And above all, I have been loved, supported, and encouraged by more people than most.

I have been blessed. It's true. I don't deny that. I have seen the hand of God at work in my life. But I have also been lucky, and I am immensely grateful for both.

Life is a mystery and there will be things we will never understand in this life. We can oversimplify them to satisfy our desire to know, but in doing so, we are only deceiving ourselves and creating illusions that will eventually need to be painfully dismantled. Or we can learn to enjoy mystery.

If we cannot learn to be comfortable with uncertainty, we cannot learn to live amidst the mess. Learning to live with not knowing is essential if we are to grow in wisdom.

This is a story I first heard thirty years ago. At the time I didn't pay much attention to it, but over time the respect the old farmer has for mystery and his detachment from outcomes have intrigued me evermore.

Once upon a time there was a farmer. He had the finest stallion in the region and the people in his village thought him very lucky to have it. One day the stallion ran away into the mountains and joined a bunch of wild horses. The farmer's neighbors gathered around saying, "Very bad luck." The farmer said, "Good luck, bad luck, who knows?"

A few days later, the stallion returned with a herd of wild horses. The neighbors gathered around saying, "Very good luck." The farmer said, "Good luck, bad luck, who knows?"

A week later the farmer's son was trying to break in one of the wild horses when he was thrown and broke his leg. The neighbors gathered around saying, "Very bad luck." The farmer said, "Good luck, bad luck, who knows?"

Several weeks later, the army came to town to recruit all able-bodied men to join the army and fight. Entering the farmer's home, they saw the boy's broken leg and left him alone. The neighbors gathered around saying, "Very good luck." The farmer said, "Good luck, bad luck, who knows?"

We want to believe that we write our own life stories, and in many ways we do, but there are also other factors and forces at play. Some of them known and some unknown, some that can be understood and others that are mysteries.

Getting unstuck.

When you experience a setback in life, or disappointment, or heartbreak, it's easy to get stuck in a rut. When our hearts are heavy, it's hard to move on.

When a car gets stuck in the mud, our instinct is to accelerate in a desperate attempt to set ourselves free. These attempts are futile. Mud flies everywhere, the car sinks deeper into the mud, and we end up with a bigger mess than we had to begin with.

We all get stuck from time to time. Sometimes we do it to ourselves, sometimes someone else does something to cause it, and sometimes circumstances conspire against us. And sometimes we get stuck because stuck is exactly where we need to be in order to pause and reflect on life.

The question is what to do when we find ourselves stuck. Albert Einstein observed, "We cannot solve problems by using the same thinking we used when we created them."

We need a new level of consciousness to get unstuck. It's one of the hardest things to attain in life. We strive for knowledge and education, but beyond these await wisdom and consciousness. The hardest thing to do in this life is to make the unconscious conscious.

From the ground floor of any of the buildings that surround Central Park it is hard to distinguish it from any other park. Go up to the tenth floor and you begin to see its scope and scale. It looks almost completely different from that vantage point. Go to the twenty-first floor and again it looks different. But it isn't. It hasn't changed, your awareness has changed. Go to the thirty-fifth floor and you will have an even greater appreciation for this spectacular greenspace in the midst of the most densely populated urban area in the United States. Fly in a helicopter over the park and you will gain new insights again.

What's going to help you get unstuck? What's going to give you a new perspective and raise your consciousness? Reading. Long walks. New friends. Old friends. Prayer. Reflection. Meditation.

What will prevent you from getting unstuck? One thing above all else: shame. Beware shame. Shame allows us to stay stuck. Enduring shame is like falling in love with being stuck.

It's okay to feel stuck. It's okay to be stuck. Just remember that you were not created to be stuck, you were created to grow. Rest a little, take some naps, cry a little, or a lot, but then listen to life pulsing through your body. You will hear that it is time, once again, to walk, to sing, to laugh, to dance, to live.

Amazing.

Everyone who really cares about you wants you to flourish. Someone who is flourishing is full of vitality. I wasn't. It is impossible for someone who is flourishing to hide it. There is a raw glow and energy that emanate from someone who is flourishing, and it is undeniable. And the thing about flourishing is, you cannot do it alone and you cannot do it for yourself. You can put yourself in situations where it is more likely to happen, but you can't make it happen.

Flourishing is beyond happiness. It is produced not only by a person's choices and actions, but also by a nurturing environment that is specifically designed to bring it about.

Human flourishing is a beautiful thing. Most of us have experienced it at some point in our lives. Maybe you flourished in math in your teens, at soccer in college, or in the third full-time job you ever had. The interesting thing is, you may have been struggling in all your other subjects, but in math, things just came together. You might have been struggling in every other area of your life, but at soccer or that particular job, everything just seemed to click.

What was different? What were you experiencing in those situations that was missing from other aspects of your life? Chances are you were uniquely supported, encouraged, challenged, and nurtured. It could have emanated from a teacher, coach, or manager. But it also could have been a study-group, teammates, or co-workers. And it could have been a combination of any or all of these. The point is: Flourishing requires an environment that is uniquely nurturing. It isn't something you can do for yourself, but it is something we can contribute to in each other.

A professional football player gets signed to a team straight out of college. Everyone who knows him is filled with great hope. In the NFL he seems like a completely different player than when he was in college. He misses plays, fumbles, and seems to be constantly in the wrong place at the wrong time. What happened? He gets traded to another team after a few seasons and again seems like a completely different player, but this time for the better, he is winning games and breaking records. What happened? It could be many things, but what is most likely to have caused such radically different results? Environment. Flourishing requires an environment that is uniquely nurturing.

Human flourishing. Isn't that what we really want? For ourselves, for our children, for our friends and spouse? And don't men and women of goodwill want this for everyone, even the people they don't know and will never meet? But what in society is set up with the specific aim of human flourishing? Does your primary relationship, your family, your social group, school, church, workplace, or neighborhood provide an environment that is uniquely nurturing? For too many people, the answer is no.

I wasn't flourishing. I knew that, but I was so focused on surviving that the idea of flourishing felt like an impossible fantasy.

When you have been traumatized by life it is natural and healthy to go through a period of intense healing and grieving. And while those processes will carry on for years, tapering off, there comes a time to return to the rigors of life. There comes a time to look to the horizon and set your course for the next phase of life. Knowing when to begin this next phase can be a challenge. But God usually sends a messenger.

It was around this time that I had an extraordinary experience. I had just finished speaking at a business conference in Palm Beach, Florida, and as I walked from the podium, I was approached by a man who wanted to speak with me. He was with a good friend of mine, so I suggested we go backstage and sit down.

"When was the last time you felt amazing?" the stranger asked as soon as I sat down.

"What do you mean?" I responded as I recovered my psychological equilibrium. The question had unsettled me. It was as if he knew something about me that I was trying really hard not to let anyone see in public.

"Well, my favorite thing about your books is the questions you ask, and that's my favorite question from all of your books."

I smiled, took a deep breath, and relaxed a little. He wasn't actually asking me when I last felt amazing, though my mind immediately started to process the question and it had been a while.

"Every day I email all my clients a question from one of your books," the man continued. "They love them. Whenever I speak to a client, we always end up talking about your questions more than we do business. Anyway, I just wanted to thank you."

He stood up, shook my hand, and disappeared.

That encounter was like a jolt straight from the heavens. It was arresting. It felt like someone had punched me in the chest to resuscitate me. It snapped me out of the cocktail of lethargy, self-pity, and sadness I was stuck in.

When was the last time I felt truly amazing? It had been a while. Sure, there had been moments, here and there, but I was searching for the last sustained period of amazing and it was concerning how far back I had to reach to find it.

There were reasons and excuses, but I knew deep down it was time to do something about it. There is a time for sowing and a time for reaping, a time to weep and a time to laugh, a time to mourn and a time to dance. It was time to dance with life again.

The following weeks were a back and forth between hope and doubt. After the most difficult seasons in our lives our hearts naturally wonder if we will ever feel amazing again. Is it even possible? It is possible, but our wounded hearts are understandably tentative.

So, let me ask you, what would have to happen for you to feel amazing?

It's time to flourish. You can't do it alone. You need an environment that is uniquely supportive. That includes people, food, sleep, exercise, prayer and reflection, feeding your mind with healthy ideas, and ridding your environment of toxicity. And don't forget: Everyone who really cares about you wants you to flourish.

A new path.

Any fool can complicate something. This is certainly true when it comes to our own lives. Too often we play the fool.

We have an astounding ability to complicate our lives in ways that empty the joy from our days.

Genius is taking something complex and making it simple. The poet Portia Nelson did that brilliantly in her *Autobiography in Five Short Chapters*. In 150 words she provides piercing insight into the journey of life. She may have written the poem about her life, but I find it captures the essence of my own. You can decide for yourself what it says about your life.

Autobiography in Five Short Chapters

I

I walk down the street.
There is a deep hole in the sidewalk.
I fall in.
I am lost . . . I am helpless.
It isn't my fault.
It takes me forever to find a way out.

II

I walk down the same street.
There is a deep hole in the sidewalk.
I pretend I don't see it.
I fall in again.
I can't believe I am in the same place
but, it isn't my fault.
It still takes a long time to get out.

III

I walk down the same street.

There is a deep hole in the sidewalk.

I see it is there.

I still fall in . . . it's a habit.

My eyes are open

I know where I am.

It is my fault.

I get out immediately.

IV

I walk down the same street.

There is a deep hole in the sidewalk.

I walk around it.

V

I walk down another street.

Are you ready to walk down another street? Are you
in a deep hole? Are you sick of falling into the same deep
hole? I am. I'm ready to walk down another street. If Portia's poem autobiography resonates with you, perhaps
you are ready to walk down another street too. This book is
about finding that other street to walk down.

There are times in our lives when we need to tweak things.
Portia describes that in chapters two, three, and four of her
poem. There are other times in life when we need decisive

and radical change. That is what she captures brilliantly in five beautifully ordinary words: "I walk down another street." Notice the simplicity of that compared to the complicated life she had been living before.

One of the most dangerous mistakes in life is to ignore the moments that invite us to walk down another street. Still, it takes tremendous awareness and courage to embrace a new direction in our lives. It is so easy to sleepwalk through life. It is so easy to keep walking down the same street, so easy to keep falling into that same hole, and all too easy to adopt the posture of the victim and blame someone else.

Life may have you in a hole. Perhaps you did it to yourself. Perhaps someone else pushed you in. Maybe it just happened. It's time to get yourself out of that hole and find a new path.

The mystery of you.

Are you ready for your new path? Maybe you are and maybe you're not. Perhaps you know what it is or perhaps the path forward has not become clear yet. Whatever path you are called to follow, whatever it is you feel called to do and become, the secret to success is diving deep into the mystery of you.

For thousands of years, humanity has been obsessed with traveling to every corner of the earth, exploring every wonder imaginable, and yet we continue to ignore, even neglect, the wonder of self.

You experience everything through the mystery of *self*. Everything. Not some things or most things, everything!

Your capacity to experience anything in life depends on how well you know your *self* and how much you are flourishing.

When you are flourishing you have more energy, and the more energy you have the more your capacity for life expands. Yes, capacity for life. That's not a small thing. Lots of people are alive, but each person's capacity for life varies. There are many things that determine our capacity for life: education, emotional intelligence, supportive family and friends, and invigorating activities, to name a few. But primary to all these is energy. Your capacity for life literally expands or contracts according to how much energy you have on any given day and in any given moment.

When was the last time you had the opportunity to do something but you simply didn't have the energy? It could have been going for a bike ride with friends or patiently explaining something to your child. But you didn't have the energy. So, you took a pass on the bike ride, and rather than teach your child how to do something, you just did it for her.

What just happened? You experienced your capacity for life being limited by your lack of energy.

It's time to flourish and in order to do that you need to investigate the mystery of you. Explore yourself bravely. Dive deep into your personal mystery.

Through this expedition you will rediscover the joy of living, the value of difficulties, the inexplicability of pain and suffering, the indispensability of love, unexpected and undeserved happiness, and the God in whom we live and move and have our being. Having rediscovered all of this, you will return to the routines and rituals of daily life with rare clarity and renewed enthusiasm.

You are a mystery worth exploring.

It always surprises me that people will travel great distances to see the wonders of this world, while all the time, the marvel of self goes unnoticed, unappreciated, unexplored, and undeveloped. It's time to change that.

The forgotten obligation.

We have so many commitments, and so many obligations. Some of them real and many of them imagined. But in the middle of all that, we often forget the obligation we have to ourselves.

You have an obligation to yourself. It makes sense when you think about it, and still, you are uncomfortable with it. In order to fulfill this obligation, you have to learn to put yourself first— not all the time, and not in a selfish way, but sometimes.

You have an obligation to yourself first. An obligation is something you are morally or legally bound to do. You are morally bound to tend to yourself. You are morally obliged to put yourself first sometimes, to take care of yourself, to ensure your needs are met in a way that allows you to thrive, so that you can live and serve powerfully. This is a moral obligation that we often neglect. And more tragically than that, it's one we rarely feel guilty about neglecting.

How you treat yourself is more crucial than how others

treat you. If you are not willing to honor the marvelous creation God made you to be, you are unlikely to demand the respect you deserve from others. In order to thrive as a human being, you need to learn to put yourself first. Before you are a mother, father, husband, wife, brother, sister, son, daughter, boyfriend, girlfriend, neighbor, colleague, you are a person first. You are a unique and wonderful individual, first.

We put ourselves first by acknowledging our legitimate needs and tending to them, encouraging ourselves, silencing our inner critic, following our passions, taking care of our health, being mindful of our strengths and talents, and being gentle with ourselves.

We need to learn new ways of putting ourselves first that lead us to flourish. The world encourages us to put ourselves first in all the wrong ways. Each morning when you wake, remember your obligation to yourself. This is the forgotten obligation.

An intimate question.

The darkest times in our lives have a way of bringing important questions to the surface. Pain and suffering demand our attention and can direct it toward areas of our lives that need adjusting. Pain asks questions, and so does suffering.

There are some questions that deserve regular reflection, but the pressures of daily life often distract us. Some questions are more intimate than others, and the more intimate the question the more likely we are to avoid it. We can avoid life's biggest questions for a long time, but only at considerable cost to our progress, happiness, and spiritual health.

The question that life stirred up in my soul at this time was a most intimate one: Do you like who you are becoming? In the depths of my despair, I realized I didn't.

When you discover that you don't like the person you are becoming you have some soul-searching to do. It was time to go within. Yes, I had suffered some cruel, even horrific betrayals, but there is no excuse for allowing these events to change me the way I did. Our lives change from the inside out. It's easy to focus on the externals, but it's what's inside that matters most.

Take an inventory.

Just about the bravest thing I have ever witnessed was a friend taking a personal inventory of his entire life. He had struggled with alcohol since he was in high school, life had brought him low, and by some grace he had decided to get help. The fourth step in the twelve steps of Alcoholics Anonymous states: *We made a searching and fearless moral inventory of ourselves.*

A moral inventory is a written objective assessment of your life, including character defects, strengths and weaknesses, and a clear-eyed look at the hurt and damage you have caused throughout your life. It's a personal history of all our transgressions. It is a completely humbling experience that breaks down our illusions. Through it we face the things we don't want to remember, the things we don't want anyone to know about us, who we have hurt and why we hurt them.

Taking a moral inventory of our entire lives, and writing it down, forces us to face things about ourselves that we conveniently tuck away deep in the recesses of our hearts and minds. But if we leave them there, they fester into fears and resentments that poison everything in our lives, especially our relationships.

A personal inventory is also a unique way to develop self-awareness. It is a life-altering experience—and you don't need to be an addict to step into this challenge. If you really want to grow spiritually, set aside a few hours three Sundays in a row, and sit down and write a searching and fearless moral inventory of yourself.

Illusions and reality.

Life's difficulties challenge our assumptions and obliterate our illusions. Our false assumptions and illusions prevent us from growing. That's why they have to be stripped away. We can strip them away ourselves, but if not, life will strip them away for us. The voluntary procedure is highly preferred over the involuntary.

An illusion is something that we have misinterpreted. It could be a false idea, a mistaken assumption, or a warped interpretation. A woman breaks up with her boyfriend, or vice versa. She explains why. But does she know herself well enough in that moment to really explain? Does she have the courage? Does he provide the atmosphere in that relationship for her to feel comfortable being completely honest? And even if all of this is true, they have each experienced the relationship differently based on past experiences, true and false assumptions, and differing priorities. The chances of him misinterpreting what she is saying are enormous, and the chances of her misinterpreting his reaction to the breakup are also significant. We misinterpret so much of what we experience.

To help us grow, reality chisels away at our illusions through the experiences of life. Some illusions we let go of easily when confronted with the evidence of reality. Others we will stubbornly cling to until our dying breath. If we cling to our illusions with sufficient rigor, they can make us physically and mentally ill.

When I first went on the road at nineteen, I was so very young—younger than my age in many ways, older in others. I had lived a sheltered life. I had been raised in my parents' love and protected by a community that cared. Setting out, I was so full of zeal, woefully naive and innocent, and ignorant about just how messy the world is.

I quickly discovered that people, and the world, were not as I had imagined. Reality demolished my illusions at first, then eroded the next layer, and still today it continues to chisel away at illusions I refuse to let go. This process forces you to acknowledge what is essential, what is trivial, and what is simply personal preference. It is when we prioritize personal preference and the trivial over what is essential and matters most that the wheels begin to fall off our lives.

Reality will always seek to obliterate our illusions, but it is for our own sake. How we respond when confronted by reality often differentiates the sane from the insane, the thriving from the struggling, and the conscious from the unconscious.

If we refuse to let go of our illusions our future possibilities narrow. And of course, those most difficult to let go of are those that have lodged deep in our unconscious. These are the illusions that have become so naturally a part of us that to suggest we part with them at first feels like a suggestion that we cut off our own right leg.

To make the onward journey we have to gradually let go of our illusions and continually embrace a little more reality each day.

The most important conversation.

The most important conversation you have each day is with yourself. It regulates self-esteem and establishes your very sense of self. Harnessing this conversation to help you become the-best-version-of-yourself is critical. Allowing it to work against you, leads you down a long, slow, steady hill toward self-pity, mediocrity, and sadness.

If you needed to radically change your life and you could change only one thing, your inner-dialogue—the way you speak to yourself—would be a very strong candidate for that change. Observe how you talk to yourself in various situations each day. Consider how this self-talk is affecting outcomes or perpetuating false assumptions. Adjust when necessary.

After you spend time with people or watch a television show, take note: Is your self-talk positive or negative? Are you speaking to yourself in a way that builds you up or tears you down? How you speak to yourself is far more impactful that how anybody else speaks to you. One of the reasons is because we always believe the things we say to ourselves, even when we are wrong. Even when they are not true.

How many beautiful, healthy women tell themselves they are fat? How many successful men tell themselves they are worthless? These illusions and dozens like them are so common they are clichés.

Choosing to spend time with people who build you up, accept you, and love you is a sign of emotional health and intelligence. But if we do not speak to ourselves in ways that are life-giving, we will not be able to receive the love, encouragement, and acceptance other people extend to us.

Be careful how you speak to yourself. Your words have power. You may never be quite able to fathom just how powerful they are. But don't waste this power. Use it wisely.

The way forward.

When pain, darkness, misfortune, and grief touch our lives, we lose our footing, get tripped up, and stumble to the ground. After we've fallen flat on our face, our instinct is to curl up in a ball physically or emotionally, or both. Getting back up can be excruciating. It may even seem impossible. We may need to rest and heal for a time, but the time will come for us to get up and continue our journey. In that moment it is crucial not to allow the long road back to overwhelm us. We just need to focus on taking the smallest step forward.

Many years ago, I went out to Colorado with a group of friends. The goal was to hike to the summit of Mount Elbert, the second highest peak in the contiguous United States. I was unprepared and it wasn't until I got out there that I discovered the others had been training. They had scheduled the hike for the day after we arrived, which I later discovered had not given us enough time to get acclimated to the altitude.

We set out in the morning, but I was quickly out of breath and struggling. I pushed myself to press on. But about a thousand feet from the summit I stopped and sat on a boulder. I couldn't go on. At least that's what my mind told me, and I believed my mind. We do that. We believe our mind, but it lies to us sometimes. Not everything your mind tells you is true.

I sat there for a while. A handful of people passed me. They were pleasant, but I wondered what they were thinking. Then, one of them stopped, turned around, and said to me, "You know, if you just keep putting one foot in front of the other, you will get there." It was obvious and simple and brilliant. One foot in front of the other. One step at a time. That was literally all I had to do to make it to the top. It's all we have to do at work, in our relationships, in our parenting, in our health, finances, and spirituality.

But we overwhelm ourselves with tomorrow's troubles, instead of focusing on today's opportunities. We look at the long journey ahead and overwhelm ourselves. But today's part of that journey is not overwhelming. It is enough—not too much, not too little. It is manageable. There is enough time today to carry out everything God wants me to. When I am stressed, anxious, and overwhelmed, I usually discover it is because I am not doing God's will but my own.

When grief and suffering touch us, when we are traumatized, life can be debilitating. The simplest task can seem completely overwhelming. In those moments, the wisdom of little by little is more valuable than ever.

This wisdom of little by little applies to every area of life. Get any group of writers together to talk about their writing process and before too long the topic of writer's block will come up. There are a thousand different theories: Go for a walk, read a favorite book, pretend writer's block doesn't exist, talk to a friend, sleep on it. The problem I find with all of these remedies, is that when you come back to write you find yourself exactly where you were when you abandoned the page. A short break may be in order, depending on how long you have been at it. But after that, write. I know it sounds crazy, but the only way out of writer's block is to write. Write anything. Skip a chapter or a section, and start writing the next chapter. Write a letter to a friend. Write whatever comes to your mind. Write about whatever you are most passionate about. Just write.

Ernest Hemingway described what he would do when he was having difficulty writing. "I would stand and look out over the roofs of Paris and think, 'Do not worry. You have always written before and you will write now. All you have to do is write one true sentence. Write the truest sentence that you know.' So finally, I would write one true sentence, and then go on from there. It was easy then because there was always one true sentence that I knew or had seen or had heard someone say."

One sentence. That's all it took to shift the momentum.

Life after you have failed, been disappointed, lost someone you love, been deceived, lost sight of who you are and what matters most, or suffered a devastating blow of the unexpected is like writer's block. You can ignore it, avoid it, pretend it isn't there, distract yourself in a million ways, but when you are done, it will still be there.

The only way out of writer's block is to write, and the only way forward in life is to live. Just as a writer will do everything to avoid writing when she has writer's block, when we have been traumatized, we will do anything to avoid living. But life is for living.

Move toward the light.

There were days when I was so traumatized that I didn't know which way was up or down, left or right, back or forward. But throughout this time, a gentle voice within kept saying, "Walk toward the light." There were days when I felt like I couldn't walk, and that voice would say, "That's okay, just move toward the light." There were days when I felt like I couldn't even move, and that voice would say, "That's okay, just look toward the light."

During those times, I became extremely sensitive to who and what was drawing me toward the light, and who and what was drawing me deeper into the darkness. And it wasn't just other people.

These are the types of things that draw me into the darkness: worry, fear, procrastination, self-destructive behavior, ruminating on the past, obsessing about the future, negative self-talk, and toxic people.

This is what draws me into the light: Prayer, reflection, meditation, reading, work, long walks, authentic love of self, acceptance of others, being loved and accepted by others, friends who want what is best for me regardless of what it costs them, and being that kind of friend to others.

What do you do when life doesn't turn out as expected? What do you do when you find yourself beat up and abandoned in one of life's dark alleys? What do you do when you have been blindsided by betrayal? Walk toward the light. There are times when we cannot distinguish between the path forward and the path back. We have become emotionally and spiritually disoriented. At those times of debilitating disorientation, be still, catch your breath. If you sense it is time to move along, but still cannot discern which path to take, move toward the light.

Find your own way. There is no one path or recipe for everyone. You have unique hopes, dreams, fears, ambitions, talents, and needs. God will use each of these to call you along your own unique path, but always toward the light.

If you're not sure where you are or what direction you should be going: move toward the light. The light always leads us forward.

One choice at a time.

One of the most pathetic things we can say as human beings is, "I had no choice." Our ability to choose is one of the things that makes us uniquely human.

As a child, I watched my father, and whenever he had a choice between doing the right thing and doing the wrong thing, he would choose the right thing. I am sure there were times when he didn't, but I was never witness to them. Situations and predicaments would arise, but his response was predictable. Whatever the right thing to do was, that's what he would do. And I must confess, there were times as a child when I wished my father were a lesser man, when I wished he wouldn't do the right thing.

My brothers and I found a soccer ball one day at the park. "Look what we found," we came home saying gleefully.

"Do you think you found it, or do you think someone lost it?" my father asked.

"Somebody lost it," one of my brothers said sheepishly.

"Come on, Dad. Please can we keep it?" another chimed in.

Dad didn't say no. He didn't say we must do this or that. He folded his newspaper and like a sage philosopher, he started asking questions, some more leading than the others, letting each question hang in the air for full-effect, and waiting for each one to be answered no matter how long it took.

"How would you feel if you had lost that soccer ball?"

"How sad do you think the boy is who saved his pocket money for weeks or months to buy that ball, who tonight is at home wondering how something so horrible could happen?"

"How will his heart sink when he remembers where he left it and comes back to find it gone?"

"If you keep it, how will that change the way that boy thinks about other people and the world?"

"If you decide to take it back, won't you teach him that the world and people are good?"

We muttered and mumbled answers to his questions. But we knew. He had taught us right from wrong. He taught us how to live. We had known as we'd walked home what our father would say.

"Better hurry back. You don't want him to get back there before you and think he has lost it forever," Dad said finally. My brothers and I walked back down the street to the park. As we walked into the park, there was a boy about nine years old, with his father, looking around the field. It was clear they were looking for the ball. We ran over and gave it to him. He was crying, tears streaming down his face.

"Thank you," his father said. "He just got it yesterday for his birthday and he was heartbroken that he had lost it." I felt the warm glow of goodness inside me, and once again I knew my father had been right.

The next day when we came home from school my father was home early from work. He was sitting at the dining room table with a brand-new soccer ball in front of him, still in its box. It was exactly the same as the one the other boy had lost. We sat down to have our afternoon snacks and my father said, "I was so proud of you boys for doing the right thing yesterday. So, I stopped by the store today and bought you a gift." My brothers and I roared with delight, gulped down our snacks, and raced out into the yard to play with the new soccer ball.

It was a powerful lesson, one of many. My father was a good man; I miss him. He taught me about life. He taught me about goodness.

We build our lives one choice at a time. Love is built one choice at a time. Character is built one choice at a time. Accomplishments are built one choice at a time. Wherever you are and wherever you feel called to go, whatever you are doing and whatever you feel called to do next, choose something today that moves you in the direction of your dreams.

However hopeless you may feel, get back in touch with your ability to choose. Remember, not all choices are equal.

We celebrate free will as if the ability to choose guarantees a good outcome. It doesn't. Some choices complicate and some simplify. Some choices bring life, and others bring death. Some bring freedom; others slavery. Some choices breed hope, while others breed despair. Some choices foster health, and others foster disease. Learn to harness the power of choice, your choices, one choice at a time, for all that is good, true, kind, noble, right, just, thoughtful, and generous.

Every moment is a chance to turn it all around. Is this your moment? Choices determine the direction of our lives. What direction is your life heading in?

Three good reasons to do anything.

The key to making good decisions is to choose what is good. It's not complicated. It's simple. Some people would say this is an over-simplification. But there is beauty, virtue, and peace of mind in choosing what is good.

Thomas Aquinas believed there were three kinds of good worth pursuing: moral good; practical good; and delightful good. These may be the only three good reasons to do anything.

Reason #1: It is morally good. Examples: love, virtue, justice.

Reason #2: It is practically necessary. Examples: eating, sleeping, working to support your family.

Reason #3: It makes you happy.

How many things did you do today that fell outside of these three reasons?

The four absolutes.

How do you make decisions? What do you measure your actions against? The four absolutes are another way to consider what to do next. In the early 1900s, the Four Absolutes were developed to help people dealing with alcoholism get their lives back.

They have been described as: a way to keep in tune with God's will for your life; moral standards; ideals to live by; yardsticks to measure our actions against; a guide for anyone trying to live the good life; and a tool for anyone trying to live intentionally.

The Four Absolutes are:

1. **Honesty.** Is it true or is it false?
2. **Unselfishness.** How will this affect other people?
3. **Purity.** Is it right or is it wrong?
4. **Love.** Is it ugly or is it beautiful?

These are powerful guides. They provide startling clarity in a confusing world. They help us to examine our options before making a decision by helping us examine our motives. This awareness is essential to spiritual growth and any form of personal development.

Consider the wisdom of the opposite. Take the first absolute for example. Lies separate us from our best self, from others, and from God. It only takes a tiny lie to put a whole universe between you and another person, or between you and God. The opposite of each of the four absolutes cause unspeakable pain and destruction every day.

How would your life be different if you adopted absolute honesty, absolute unselfishness, absolute purity, and absolute love? I am not proposing these need to be everyone's guide, but if not these, what yardstick do you use to measure your actions and make decisions?

A personal philosophy.

Philosopher means "lover of wisdom." The most practical application of any philosophy is that it empowers people to make decisions. If someone does you wrong, how do you respond? Some philosophies propose revenge; others justice; and some forgiveness.

Do you have a philosophy by which you choose to live?

I am a Christian. I believe Jesus' teachings are the best way to live. Even if you could prove to me that Jesus never existed, I would still believe that his teachings propose the best way to live. I have studied other religions and philosophies and that is the conclusion I have reached. What I love about Jesus' teachings is that they apply to everyone, everywhere, in every situation. They are not elitist, but accessible to all. Imagine for a moment how the world would be different if everyone *strove* to live these teachings. Imagine how much of the world's suffering would be eradicated.

The teachings of Jesus are many, so throughout my day,

when I have a decision to make, I simply ask myself: Will this help me become the-best-version-of-myself? This question always brings clarity. This is my personal philosophy; it is drawn from my belief that God created all men and women to become the-best-version-of-themselves. This is God's dream for us, and our dream for anyone we truly love. My experience of life has led me to discover that I am fully alive when I am striving to become all God created me to be. There is no other way to be fully alive.

How do you make decisions? Do you have a process? Do you have guiding principles? Do you have a personal philosophy?

Without a personal philosophy, life can seem confusing and complex, because every time you have a decision to make, you need to build a philosophy from scratch. This becomes exhausting, and decisions made when we are exhausted are rarely good ones. When we are tired, stressed, or in destress a personal philosophy is especially helpful. These scenarios make it harder for the mind to reach decisions, because our clarity is compromised.

In addition to helping you make better decisions, the most practical advantage to having a personal philosophy is that it empowers you to make decisions with speed, clarity, and confidence.

Become a lover of wisdom, a philosopher. This will help you become a great decision maker. Be able to look back on your life three months from now, a year from now, ten years from now and identify the wisest decisions you have made and the fruit they bore in your life. Make wisdom a priority in your life, and watch your life flourish.

The world needs whole generations of philosophers to rescue it from the path it is on. May we all become lovers of wisdom.

The wisdom of simplicity.

Would you describe your life as beautifully simple or tragically complicated? The wisest men and women of every age have valued simplicity, while the average person falls unknowingly into a dozen complications every day.

Albert Einstein was one of the greatest geniuses of all time. He observed that "Genius is taking the complex and making it simple." Perhaps it's time to apply this genius to our lives.

William of Ockham was a fourteenth-century philosopher and logician. He is best known for his problem-solving principle known as Occam's razor: "The *simplest solution* is almost always the *best*." For seven hundred years, this theory has been guiding the great thinkers of every discipline. Genius and simplicity have become inseparable among the wisest people of every culture. Still, in a world with unlimited options, we struggle to adopt and apply the wisdom of simplicity to daily life.

Henry David Thoreau observed, "I believe in simplicity. It is astonishing as well as sad, how many trivial affairs even the wisest thinks he must attend to in a day; how singular an affair he thinks he must omit. When the mathematician would solve a difficult problem, he first frees the equation of all incumbrances, and reduces it to its simplest terms. So, simplify the problem of life, distinguish the necessary and the real."

Every day you face hundreds of choices, options, and decisions. We fall into complexity by default, and complexity has an unerring habit of creating a mess or adding to the mess. Allow yourself to be governed by a quest for simplicity. Most people don't. Not because this doesn't make sense, but because we don't spend enough time reflecting on life. We spend more time planning our annual vacation than we do considering our lives.

Adopt the wisdom of simplicity. You will never be sorry you did. Apply it to every aspect of your life. It is an excellent path to clarity and peace. The beautiful minds of every age have cherished simplicity. Follow their genius.

Simple living is the essence of wisdom. The desire for simplicity itself is a sign of wisdom. If you are stuck, the most natural way to get unstuck is to simplify your life, strip away everything that is not essential. To move forward you need clarity, and simplicity gives birth to clarity.

Still not convinced? Here are nine reasons to simplify your life:

1. **Meaning.** Simplicity leads to a more meaningful life. The secret to living a meaningful life is to strip away everything that is meaningless. Strip away anything

that is trivial or unnecessary and everything left will be meaningful.

2. **Time.** The wisdom of simplicity teaches you to say no. This gives you more free time, more time for what matters most.

3. **Relationships.** If you want your relationships to thrive, choose simplicity in all things. This will create time to be with each other, and all relationships thrive when you give them carefree timelessness.

4. **Clarity.** Adopting the wisdom of simplicity will lead to greater clarity about who you are and what matters most. This will lead you to make better decisions. With the clarity of simplicity you will continue to eliminate anything that is unnecessary, shifting the focus of your life from the trivial many to the essential few.

5. **Fulfillment.** The simple life is more fulfilling. When we rush around tasting everything, but savoring nothing, we become dissatisfied and unfulfilled. Simplicity allows us to drink deeply and savor the most important things in life. To savor is to taste and enjoy completely. When was the last time you savored something?

6. **Freedom.** Simplicity is liberating. Complexity is a form of slavery. Simplicity literally makes us free. Money, things, and commitments take up space in our minds and complicate our lives. Liberate yourself from commitments and unnecessary possessions, simplify your life, and little by little, you will liberate yourself.

7. **Integrity.** Simplicity makes it a little easier to live in alignment with your values. Living a simple life creates fewer situations in which your values are challenged. When we complicate our lives, we end up with "the end justifies the means" thinking. When we abandon our values, we abandon ourselves, and, separated from ourselves we can never be happy.

8. **Needs.** Simple living is the secret to abundance. The wisdom of simplicity helps you realize that your needs are infinitely more important than your wants. We need so little; keep your wants simple. Socrates observed that the richest man is not he who has the most, but he who needs the least.

9. **Less.** Less really is more—and better!

The simple life is one of the few things in life that doesn't disappoint. Which of these nine things don't you want? Is there anything you want more than these? So why do we keep complicating our lives? Why isn't simplicity one of our core values?

How does life get so complicated?

If you really want to embrace the simple life, you need to know how life gets so complicated in the first place. We complicate our lives unnecessarily in a thousand ways, chasing things we neither need nor really want. Swept along by a culture of expectations, most people never pause long enough to reflect upon the deepest desires of their hearts.

If we are going to celebrate simplicity, it's important to understand how our lives get complicated. We are not victims of complication. We run willingly into the arms of complication. We complicate life. Sometimes it is the result of one big decision and sometimes it is the result of a thousand little decisions. There are times when the unexpected events of life bring chaos and complexity, though it is usually their addition to the chaos and complexity we have already created that makes life stressful or even seemingly unbearable.

We complicate our lives in many ways. Most people can come up with a list. But there is one thing we rarely consider when examining why our lives have become so complicated.

My father was a businessman. He taught me many things about personal finances and the life and responsibilities of an entrepreneur. One of the lessons I will never forget was about purchasing things. He used to talk about two costs: the first and the second cost. The cost to purchase something, and the cost to maintain it. It's the cost to maintain a car, a home, or any valuable asset that often gets people into trouble. And the more expensive something is, the more expensive it typically is to maintain. So, when you buy a car, you are not making a single purchase decision, but dozens. In that one decision, you are also deciding to purchase gas for the car, service it regularly, buy new tires when needed, repair it if you have an accident or it gets vandalized, and other things you may not even be aware of at the time. This is the compounding effect of choice.

Since my father explained the two costs, I have learned that there is also a third cost. The third cost is time. Everything we buy requires time.

One day Doug and Susie decided to get a dog. They knew it was a big decision, but they both had dogs growing up and they thought they were ready.

Read the previous sentence and see if you can find the error. Here it is: *They knew it was a big decision.* It wasn't a big decision. It was a thousand decisions. More actually.

The average life expectancy of a dog is around twelve years. Ideally, dogs should relieve themselves outside three times a day. So, the choice to get a dog is also 13,140 pre-made decisions to take the dog out to pee. If someone said to you, "Could you take my dog out to pee thirteen thousand times?" what would you say?

Getting a dog is a hundred thousand decisions, which means you are saying no to a hundred thousand other things. When people decide to get a dog, they are vaguely aware of what is involved, but the great majority have never considered everything that is involved. They don't consider that they are choosing to take that dog out for a pee more than thirteen thousand times. And this is just one aspect of a dog's life and the responsibilities of its owner. There is also food, checkup visits to the vet, puppy classes, and registering your dog. This is all before the dog gets sick, which he or she eventually will. But we don't think about these things when we are making that one decision.

The offset, of course, is the joy the dog will bring you and your family. This is what we focus on when making the decision. Don't get me wrong—I love puppies as much as the next person, but my first goal here is to give an example of how what we think is a single decision can actually lead to a thousand premade choices and commitments. My ultimate goal here is to encourage us all to reach for a higher level of consciousness when we are making decisions.

The mistake we make is that we think getting a puppy is one choice. Not so. One choice made freely can lead to a thousand obligations, or even a million slaveries, depending on the situation.

E.B. White perfectly encapsulated this idea with staggering clarity in *Charlotte's Web* when he wrote, "There's no limit to how complicated things can get on account of one thing always leading to another."

Simplicity is a thing of beauty as John Keats would say. Simplicity is found in truth, beauty, goodness, and justice. It is highly desired, but rarely sought. Only you can decide if you will adopt the true love of simplicity or be seduced by the illusions of complexity.

Unless simplicity is a goal, one that we work to accomplish and defend relentlessly, our lives will increasingly become complex, overwhelming, and unmanageable. One thing always leads to another... if we let it. Allow the wisdom of simplicity to guide each decision you make.

Learn to say no.

No is your friend when it comes to embracing simplicity. In fact, no is your friend when it comes to implementing most of the lessons on these pages are stirring within you. Most of us know we need to get better at saying no, so I am not going to wax lyrical on the subject. I will just say this one thing and invite you to reflect upon it: *If you are not free to say no, you aren't free to say yes.*

Work on being free to say no and your yes will be more focused, meaningful, and powerful than ever before. What you say yes to determines everything. And if you don't say no to the wrong things there will be no room in your life to say yes to the right things.

We say we want to live more meaningful lives, but we keep saying yes to meaningless things. Start saying no to meaningless things and allow a life of meaning and fulfillment to emerge within and around you.

The main threat to your wholeness.

If something was threatening your happiness, would you want to know about it? If people knew you could never be truly whole without something and they withheld that information from you, how would you feel?

The greatest threat to your happiness and wholeness is your unrecognized spiritual needs.

That's thirteen words that took me a lifetime to formulate. It's an idea that I have known, forgotten, and remembered again too many times to count. I mean it with all sincerity, that if you sat with that single sentence for thirty minutes every day for a year, pondering, reflecting, wondering, meditating upon what it means to you, it would be time well spent.

You are a spiritual being. Life is not just a physical experience. It's clear that it is also an emotional experience, and an intellectual experience, but we neglect the *reality* that it is also a spiritual experience. We are obsessed with the physical aspect of self, while ignoring the spiritual aspect. You cannot live life to the fullest if you ignore your spiritual self. You cannot be fully alive without spirituality. You cannot thrive and flourish while letting your soul starve.

Today's culture has embraced the illusion that spirituality is an optional extra. But our spiritual needs have not diminished and are not being met. We each bear the responsibility to seek and find the spiritual nourishment we need for the next league of our journey.

If I live for another hundred years, I may never write a line so full of meaning as this: The greatest threat to your happiness and wholeness is your unrecognized spiritual needs.

A spiritual experience.

There is no substitute for a vibrant spiritual life. A rich inner life is essential to human flourishing. If we want to live life to the fullest, we need to give priority to the spiritual aspect of who we are.

"I am not a spiritual person," some people say. It's not true.

It's a denial of reality, a delusion that will continue to clash with reality until alignment is reached. It's like saying there is no such thing as gravity.

In the late 1920s, Rowland Hazard III visited the pioneering psychoanalyst Carl Jung in Switzerland. Hazard was a successful American businessman and a hopeless alcoholic who had required hospitalization on more than one occasion. Having exhausted other treatments and remedies, he was desperate to get well. Jung worked with Rowland intensely for an unknown period of time, but the American returned again to the excesses of alcohol. There are stories that after departing from Jung's care, he stopped at the first bar and got drunk. His compulsion for alcohol was so great that Jung finally declared that at that time Rowland was immune to psychological treatment. The simple question Rowland then asked was, "Is there no hope, then?"

"No, there is none—except that some people with your problem have recovered if they have a transforming spiritual experience," was the doctor's answer.

What was Jung saying? Without a spiritual experience there is no hope. Without a spiritual experience you will not get healthy.

What was true for Rowland Hazard is true for you and me. *I'm not an alcoholic*, you may be thinking. You may not even drink alcohol. It doesn't matter. We all need to overcome something, we all need to recover from something, in order to make the onward journey.

This reminds me of an often-neglected passage in the Bible. In Mark's Gospel there is a story of a man who brings his son, who is possessed by a demon, to Jesus' disciples and asks them to heal him. The disciples had been successful healing people and casting out demons using the method Jesus had taught them. But in this case, they were unable to help the boy. Jesus comes along and casts out the demon himself. Later his disciples question him, asking why they were not able to heal the boy. Jesus replies, "Some evil spirits can only be cast out by prayer and fasting" (Mark 9:29).

Fasting is a powerful spiritual practice that is engaged not to punish the self, but to liberate it. But in our comfort-obsessed world it has fallen out of use. The combination of prayer and fasting has an impeccable record of creating transformative spiritual experiences for thousands of years. In a sense, Jung was echoing what Jesus had already made known.

But remember Rowland's question: Is there no hope? Anytime you get to a place of hopelessness or find yourself on a path that seems to be leading there, seek out a "transforming spiritual experience." Don't wait for a powerful spiritual experience to come to you. Seek it out. Go looking for it. The best way to predict the future is to create it. The best way to create it is in collaboration with God.

I understand why many have rejected religion. I have met too many people with deep faith wounds not to understand. Still, rejecting something you need to thrive makes no sense. We are spiritual beings in need of spiritual sustenance. Feed your soul. Spiritual experiences are essential for your well-being. A spiritual outlook and a vibrant daily spirituality are crucial to the overall flourishing of each and every human being.

Remember: the greatest threat to your happiness and wholeness is your unrecognized spiritual needs.

Three appointments.

We are all required to keep three appointments. The appointment with self, the appointment with God, and the inevitable appointment with death. We may avoid, deny, resist, ignore, and otherwise pretend that these appointments are not on our schedule. It matters not. Life brings about these appointments whether we think we are ready or not.

The first appointment is with self. It's amazing how we avoid ourselves. Few things contribute more to our collective sense that something is missing and that we are living someone else's life than the avoidance of self.

Long ago, I learned to keep a daily appointment with self. Unless I check-in with myself each day, I will eventually betray myself in small ways and large. But when I keep this appointment, I emerge with a clear and firm sense of self. This sense of self—knowing who we are and what we are here for—is more precious than gold.

The quality of all our relationships is determined by the quality of our relationship with ourselves. This is one of the many reasons the first appointment is critical. When we avoid this appointment, we limit all of our relationships.

The second appointment is with God. We avoid God, run from him, thinking that we want something other than what he wants to give us. But in running from God, we run from ourselves. Alienation from God is alienation from self. Only in union with God do we discover and become our truest self.

When we discover how messy and difficult life is, we hear an urgent call to remake and rebuild the inner life. What was once an invitation quickly turns into a summons. Not the summons of a tyrannical God that demands we pay attention, but rather, the summons of our own soul to pay attention before it wilts and dies.

Turn to God each day for some period of time. Who else will lead you to green pastures and peaceful waters? Who else will make your cup overflow? Who else will restore your soul?

I don't know about you, but I need that. My soul needs to be restored.

The third appointment is with death. It is the inescapable truth. It is a non-negotiable assignment. Jack Nicholson is walking through a bar when he recognizes someone he knows. He doesn't stop, but he slows down. "How are you?" he asks. The guy begins to complain about something and Jack cuts him off, "We're all dying. Act accordingly." Is it blunt? Yes. Is it true? Yes. We are all dying, but we don't act accordingly.

"Every man dies, but not every man really lives," was William Wallace's observation. Nobody fears death more than those who have not lived. Nobody fears death more than those who have not discovered who they are and offered that gift to the world. Death is inevitable, but a well-lived life is not.

When you come to the end of your life, when death is undeniably near, what will bring you unmitigated joy? Thinking about death is morbid some may say. I disagree. Far from being unhealthy, it is a valuable and meaningful exercise. Thinking too much about death can be morbid, but how much is too much? I suggest that you think about death only as much as is necessary to live life to the fullest.

When we are young it feels like we have all the time in the world. But we don't. Sooner than we expect, we begin to slow down. We can't do the things we used to be able to do. All the time our bodies are breaking down, though we often don't acknowledge it until we get sick or are dying. How will you feel when you are dying? What will you think? It is an appointment we all must keep. Don't arrive unprepared.

If you found out today that you were dying, what would be your regrets? What do those regrets tell you about how you are living your life? What changes do those regrets invite you to make?

The wisest people of every age have pondered death and eternity. Not as an exercise in morbidity, but in order to live life to the fullest.

Death and the knowledge of its inevitability serve an important purpose in our lives. Imagine how carelessly and recklessly people would live if they knew they would live forever in this world.

If living a meaningful life depends on filling our lives with meaningful activity, these three appointments should figure regularly on our schedule. These three appointments help us to weed out the meaningless from the meaningful. They help us prioritize what matters most and give us the courage to say no to what matters least. They build within us a true sense of self, and few things are more important. These three appointments, in short, keep us alert and aware of our blessings, help us to become more perfectly ourselves, and live life to the fullest.

Speak up.

When we are traumatized, we often lose our voice. If trauma could speak it would say things like: "Shut-up!" "What you think doesn't matter." "Your voice isn't important." "Nobody cares about you." "Your pain is irrelevant." "You will never recover from this."

Trauma doesn't have a voice, but these are the kinds of things we feel when we are traumatized. So, after we have been hurt, manipulated, abused, betrayed, deceived—after we have had our hearts, minds, bodies, and souls broken—learning to find our voice is harder and yet more important than ever.

The obvious occurred to me as I began to recover: Good people want to hear what you have to say. If you don't open your mouth, you will not be heard. People can't hear your thoughts or read your mind. If you don't ask, the answer will always be no. If you don't let people know what you need, your needs will go unmet.

To need is to be profoundly human. We need. To think otherwise is to go beyond illusion and enter into delusion. We need air to breathe, water to drink, food to eat, to be touched and held, to love and be loved, opportunities to learn new things, and second chances. We need. To need is to be human, and life cannot be an amazing experience if you deny your humanity. This is the most tragic way we dehumanize ourselves.

So, speak up. You don't need to be obnoxious about it, but you will feel set free when you do. And the amazing thing is, the people who really love you want to hear what you have to say. They will be fascinated and enamored.

A bad bargain.

To get unstuck we have to stop making bad bargains. What's a bad bargain? When you *lose* more than you gain. I'm not saying the goal in life should be to always get more than you give. *Lose* is the word I used. Losing something is different than *giving* generously. And *taking* is something altogether different again. It's time to stop making bad bargains with yourself, others, and life.

Let's talk about the first and the worst. The first bad bargain we make is when we complicate our lives. When we complicate our lives, we always lose more than we gain.

The worst bad bargain you make is anytime you pretend you are someone other than your own wonderful self. If you have to be less than yourself for someone to like you, care about you, love you, or want to work with you—you are losing more than you are gaining and making a bad bargain.

Are you on the cusp of making another bad bargain? Step back and reconsider.

Forgiveness.

There is no path forward without forgiveness. I know that. Still, forgiving is one of the hardest things to do in this life. And the more you love someone, and the more that person hurts you, the harder it is to forgive.

I am not good at it. I won't pretend I am. Still, I try. I struggle to forgive. It's easy to say the words, but then you have to live them. Some days I feel I am making great progress, and then there are days when I am being tossed about in the tornado of regression. There are times when I am certain that I have forgiven someone—this belief may last for weeks, months—but then I discover another piece of shrapnel in my heart and I find myself needing to forgive again, in new and deeper ways. What I find humbling is that it is my need to forgive, not their need to be forgiven. The person could be long gone and no longer a part of my life. He may not have even thought of me in years.

The need is mine, and I find it is healthy to remember that.

The spirit is willing, but my wounded heart holds onto the hurt. It doesn't realize it is holding on to poison. The man in me understands, but the little boy in me is still paralyzed by the injuries.

Forgiveness requires incredible strength. It requires divine assistance. But you don't need all the strength at once, just a little at a time.

When I am struggling to forgive, this is my prayer. This is what I ask God.

Spirit of God,
At this time,
I am unable or unwilling to forgive.
I know not which.
Fill me with the wisdom of forgiveness.
Bring me to the beautiful truth
that forgiving others is part of my own healing.
Cleanse me of the poison of unforgiveness.
Shine light so I can see how unforgiveness
affects my physical, emotional, and spiritual health.
Today,
I am unable or unwilling to forgive.
I know not which.
Just give me the desire to forgive.
Just the desire.
This is all I ask today.

Give me the desire to forgive.
For I know, trust, and believe,
that if you place the desire to forgive
firmly in my heart,
that desire will grow,
and the day will come
when I am both willing and able to forgive.
Amen.

Whom do you need to forgive? It's okay if you are not there yet. Be patient with yourself. Just don't quit and allow your heart to become hardened. I know it's not easy, but there is no path forward without forgiveness. And whomever you need to forgive, and whatever you need to forgive them for, is not worth preventing your onward journey.

There is no future without forgiveness.

Change something.

Why are we so complacent, even indifferent, about our own lives?

Many years ago, I heard a powerful story from a friend in Australia. The story had an immediate impact on me, but it took on bold new meaning during this time in my life.

Clare grew up in Australia before moving to the United States and getting married. Each year she saved every penny she could to go home to Australia for a month with her son. During that month, she would visit her relatives; she especially looked forward to spending time with her brother John.

John loves his sister and would do anything for her. But year after year, the sister who returned was different from the year before... and very different from the sister he remembered growing up with. After several years, John decided he needed to do something or say something, but he didn't know what. On the last day of Clare's visit that year, he invited her to take a drive with him. They drove around for a while talking about lots of things, and then John pulled the car over to the side of the road.

Turning to his sister, he told her how much he loved her, that he wanted her to be happy, and he shared how he was growing more concerned each year with how her life was unfolding. Clare's eyes began to fill with tears. "You just don't seem happy, sis!" he said. "You are less and less of a person each year." Clare just sat there as a single tear escaped her left eye, ran down her cheek, and splashed on her thigh just below the line of her summer dress.

"You deserve to be happy, sis!" John continued and Clare nodded knowingly. "I don't know what to do or say. I just wish I could help you, but I think this is something you have to do for yourself."

Clare finally spoke saying, "I just feel stuck, lost, angry..."

"I know you do," John empathized with her. "Just promise me you'll do something different this year. I know Mom and Dad and your friends all have their opinions about what you should do, but I am not going to get into that. Only you can decide what it's going to be. Just change something. I'm not going to tell you what you should change. Just promise me you will change something. Take some time to think about what you need to do, and then, just flip that switch. Promise me."

Clare nodded and cried some more, and now John began to cry too. But the conversation itself had already flipped a switch for Clare. She knew what she needed to do, and a very different Clare returned to Australia the following year.

Now it is your turn, and mine. Promise me you will change something. There is no need to be rash or impulsive, but promise me when you work out what it is you will flip that switch. This is a new springtime in your life. It's time for a new path. Have the courage to make the change, flip the switch, and you will look back a year from now with awe and amazement.

When change seems too daunting.

The messiness of life can be paralyzing. When we most need change, we often feel least capable of embracing the change we know we desperately need. But that's okay.

Imagine the smallest adjustment you could make to your life. Something tiny. So small it seems insignificant. Liken it to turning and facing in the right direction at the beginning of a journey of a thousand miles. That's right, not even the first step, just turning and facing in the right direction. If that's all you can manage right now, it's enough. Just don't let what you can't do interfere with what you can.

When change seems too daunting, just make a small adjustment, and pay attention to how your energy shifts and your spirits rise.

The basics.

Imagine for a moment that you were injured in an accident and you had to learn to walk and talk again. It would be excruciating. Each half step, each syllable, requiring all your concentration and effort. And then, there is the mental anguish of not-knowing if you will ever walk again or talk again. Recovering from any trauma is like learning to walk again. It is slow and can be excruciatingly painful and difficult. Be patient with yourself. Be gentle with yourself. Celebrate every advance no matter how small.

Gently down the stream.

As children we are taught many of life's most important lessons, but as we grow older, we discard them as childish and useless.

The nursery rhyme *Row, Row, Row Your Boat* is but one example. It consists of one verse, made up of eighteen words, which repeats. This repetition is hypnotizing and hopes we will remember its lessons all our lives. "Keep it simple" is perhaps the first lesson.

Row, row, row your boat

Gently down the stream
Merrily, merrily, merrily, merrily
Life is but a dream

What thoughts cross your mind as you read the lyrics? Which words jump out at you as you read them? When did you last live a single day that reflects the wisdom of the rhyme?

Here is my stream of consciousness: **Row.** You have to row. There is effort involved. It's not float or drift. **Your boat.** We are each responsible for our own boat. I am not responsible for rowing your boat, nor you mine. **Gently.** This is a calm activity; there is no thrashing or racing. **Down.** It's not about battling to get upstream. **Down the stream.** There is direction; we are not aimlessly drifting. **Merrily.** Cheerful, relaxed, enjoying the present moment. This one verse of the song has more merrily than some weeks of my life. When was the last time I experienced this merrily? I am not a very merrily person. What is merrily? Cheerful, I think. Why am I not more cheerful? What prevents me from being more cheerful? **Life is but a dream.** Don't take everything so seriously. Life passes quickly.

What lesson do you take away from the exercise? There are two for me: Slow down and be gentle with yourself. The speed of our lives can be a form of violence. Being excessively busy can be a form of violence. I wonder why I treat myself so poorly sometimes. I need to practice "gently down the stream" and "merrily, merrily, merrily, merrily."

Becoming real.

The books our parents and grandparents read to us in childhood are filled with a lifetime of profound insight. They contain beautiful, important truths; ten-thousand years of collective wisdom. These messages bind to our subconscious and emerge throughout our lives when we need them most.

When I was a child, my mother used to read me *The Velveteen Rabbit*. This was the book that emerged from my sub-conscious during these times of my adulthood. These are the enduring messages that continue to captivate me:

"The Skin Horse had lived longer in the nursery than any of the others. He was so old that his brown coat was bald in patches and showed the seams underneath, and most of the hairs in his tail had been pulled out to string bead necklaces. He was wise, for he had seen a long succession of mechanical toys arrive to boast and swagger, and by-and-by break their mainsprings and pass away, and he knew that they were only toys, and would never turn into anything else. For nursery magic is very strange and wonderful, and only those playthings that are old and wise and experienced like the Skin Horse understand all about it."

"What is REAL?" asked the Rabbit one day, when they were lying side by side near the nursery fender, before Nana came to tidy the room. "Does it mean having things that buzz inside you and a stick-out handle?"

"Real isn't how you are made," said the Skin Horse. "It's a thing that happens to you. When a child loves you for a long, long time,

not just to play with, but REALLY loves you, then you become Real."

"Does it hurt?" asked the Rabbit.

"Sometimes," said the Skin Horse, for he was always truthful. "When you are Real you don't mind being hurt."

"Does it happen all at once, like being wound up," the Rabbit asked, "or bit by bit?"

"It doesn't happen all at once," said the Skin Horse. "You become. It takes a long time. That's why it doesn't happen often to people who break easily, or have sharp edges, or who have to be carefully kept. Generally, by the time you are Real, most of your hair has been loved off, and your eyes drop out and you get loose in the joints and very shabby. But these things don't matter at all, because once you are Real you can't be ugly, except to people who don't understand."

"I suppose you are Real?" said the Rabbit. And then he wished he had not said it, for he thought the Skin Horse might be sensitive. But the Skin Horse only smiled.

"The Boy's Uncle made me Real," he said. "That was a great many years ago; but once you are Real you can't become unreal again. It lasts for always."

"Weeks passed, and the little Rabbit grew very old and shabby, but the Boy loved him just as much. He loved him so hard that he loved all his whiskers off, and the pink lining to his ears turned grey, and his brown spots faded. He even began to lose his shape, and he scarcely looked like a rabbit anymore, except to the Boy. To him he was always beautiful, and that *was all that the little Rabbit cared about. He didn't mind how he looked to other people, because the nursery magic had made him Real, and when you are Real shabbiness doesn't matter."*

Perhaps all that has been happening to me, within me, has just been helping me to become real. But it does hurt, and unlike the Skin Horse, I do mind being hurt.

Run toward yourself.

There are few things worse than feeling alienated from yourself. When life drags you down, one of the things you realize quickly is how you have neglected yourself. What does it mean to neglect something? You fail to care for it properly. This is one of those holes I keep falling in. It is a very specific example of how "Autobiography in Five Short Chapters" applies to me. Is self-neglect a hole you keep falling into also? Go back and read the poem one more time with this in mind.

There is one method I found confronting and useful. It never fails to align me with self, though it can be astoundingly difficult to practice some days, which may sound strange when you hear how simple the exercise is. But it is a true testament to the fact that just because something is simple doesn't mean it is easy.

Here it is: At the beginning of each day, stand in front of a mirror, look yourself directly in the eye, and listen to what the man or woman—in the mirror says to you. This will make you uncomfortable. But it works. Your eyes will tell you something every single day of your life if you listen.

What type of things will your eyes say? You know what you need to do. They are not listening to you. It's time for something new. Go for a walk today. You are a good person. Today is going to be a great day, try to enjoy it. You are not paying attention to your needs. You should go and see your doctor. This has to stop. Don't let them walk all over you like that. You need some time off. Your critics don't know you well enough to compliment you or criticize you. A true friend would never treat you that way. Call your mom. Do something to make someone else's day today.

Run toward yourself by listening to the man, or woman, in the mirror.

The guy in the glass.

In 1934, the American writer Dale Wimbrow wrote this poem. It has often been misquoted and misattributed, but its message endures.

The Guy in the Glass

When you get what you want in your struggle for pelf,
And the world makes you King for a day,
Then go to the mirror and look at yourself,
And see what that guy has to say.
For it isn't your Father, or Mother, or Wife,

Who judgement upon you must pass.
The feller whose verdict counts most in your life
Is the guy staring back from the glass.

He's the feller to please, never mind all the rest.
For he's with you clear up to the end,
And you've passed your most dangerous, difficult test
If the guy in the glass is your friend.

You may be like Jack Horner and "chisel" a plum,
And think you're a wonderful guy,
But the man in the glass says you're only a bum
If you can't look him straight in the eye.

You can fool the whole world down the pathway of years,
And get pats on the back as you pass,
But your final reward will be heartaches and tears
If you've cheated the guy in the glass.

Character is destiny.

The Greek philosopher Heraclitus observed, "Character is destiny." I kept reminding myself of this during those dark days.

Character can be acquired intentionally, by proactively developing habits of the heart, mind, body, and soul. It can also be acquired passively by enduring life's inconveniences, difficulties, and unavoidable suffering. But there are no shortcuts. You cannot hack your way to character. It is the greatest investment you can make in yourself.

What is character? It's getting harder and harder to get people to agree on a definition. Some say it's working hard and being honest. Others say it's doing what you say you will do. Many agree that it is living in alignment with your values. But what if you work hard in a criminal enterprise? What if you are honest about the manipulative intentions you have? What if what you say you will do is hateful and hurtful? And what if your values are anger, revenge, selfishness, and pleasure above all else? I doubt many would conclude that living out these values reflects high character.

So, what is character? It's moral excellence. But we don't talk about morality anymore. When did you last participate in a conversation aimed at exploring if something was moral or not? When was the last time you heard someone described as a person of high moral character? Where could someone go if they wanted to learn about moral excellence?

In the chokehold of relativism, we have become confused about the difference between right and wrong—so confused, that we are not even sure right, wrong, good, and bad even exist.

But surely it is wrong for a person to spend his life in prison for a crime he did not commit. Can we agree that is wrong? More than a million men, women, and children are victims of human trafficking across international borders every year. Can we all agree that is bad and wrong? It is impossible to build character without a sense of right, wrong, good, bad, just, and unjust.

One of the most ludicrous debates in our society over the past twenty years has been about character. Does character matter? The mere fact that we are asking this question means that we have lost our way.

Character is destiny. This is true for a person, a marriage, a family, and yes, for a nation. What does our future look like if that is true? Maybe it's time to place character back at the center of our families, communities, and education system. Whatever it is we wish to rebuild in our lives and in our nation, let us begin with character.

How do you build character? With virtue. Virtues are the building blocks of character. Think about this short list of virtues: patience, kindness, humility, gentleness, perseverance, truthfulness, courage, temperance, justice, faithfulness, and goodwill. Would your life improve if you had more of these virtues, in both number and degree? Would you be a better spouse? Would you be a better parent? A better sibling, friend, colleague, neighbor, and citizen?

I've tried a hundred different ways to improve my life. They didn't work. The only way to genuinely improve your life is with virtue. You cannot improve your life in any meaningful way without improving as a human being. Any improvement that does not come from expanding your potential as a human being is cosmetic.

Virtue is also the only way for a society to make genuine

progress. Progress built on anything other than character and virtue is a mirage.

I love being around people of high character. They stoke my desire to grow, expand, improve. I am fascinated with great accomplishments, but I respect virtue. Accomplishment is infinitely easier than virtue. I love being around virtuous people. They make me want to be a better person.

People of exceptional character put character first. They put it above everything else. It doesn't matter what it costs them, because they know that to abandon character would be to lose their very self.

If to lose character is to lose self, then the path to finding self is also character. If you want to discover yourself, dedicate yourself to growing in a very specific virtue each month. As we grow in virtue, we grow in character; and as we grow in character, we come to know our truest self.

Character is not some generic, boring, rule-abiding, cookie-cutter thing. It is personal and dynamic; it manifests differently and beautifully in every person. So, together, let us place character and virtue at the center of daily living. Surround yourself with people who are striving for virtue and character. And beware anyone who is incapable of delaying gratification. It is a sure sign that virtue has been banished from someone's life.

Alignment issues.

If you have ever driven a car that has alignment issues, you know how uncomfortable, stressful, and dangerous it can be. The same is true when our lives get knocked out of alignment. Life becomes uncomfortable, stressful, dangerous, and riddled with anxiety.

When things are aligned, they are in the correct arrangement in relation to everything else. It's interesting how much time we spend putting our material possessions in the right place. It's easier than tidying up our souls, and easier than aligning our actions with our values.

The challenge of living consciously, ethically, morally, is to align our thoughts, words, and actions, with our purpose and values. When our actions fall out of alignment with our values, the wheels begin to wobble.

If your words, thoughts, and actions don't align with what's in your heart you will never have peace. So much of our stress, unhappiness, and anxiety, is caused when our lives fall out of alignment with our highest values.

Stress, unhappiness, anxiety, and depression are not bad things. They are not human malfunctions. Quite the opposite, they are proof that everything is working as it should. They come to us as messengers, to tap us on the shoulder and point out that our lives have slipped out of alignment.

We are most fully human, and most fully alive, when we are living an integrated life. This is integrity: aligning our actions with what we know to be good, true, just, and right.

When we turn our backs on what is good, true, just, and right, when we abandon our highest values, our integrity gets eroded. This always results in a loss of self, great or small. When our integrity is being eroded, you can be sure a number of other things are happening too. We are losing sight of who we are and what we value. We are losing our sense of self, which leads to an identity crisis. But all along the way, we are hurting people, often the people we claim to love the most, and always ourselves.

Misalignment always leads to pain and suffering for you and for others. What area of your life is misaligned? It takes boldness to admit it. How do you realign your life and live with more integrity than ever before? One decision at a time. Move your heart and mind into agreement, and act out of that united self.

Measuring your life.

From time to time, we weigh our lives. Sometimes we are satisfied with what we discover, sometimes we are disappointed, and sometimes we are concerned. But it is good to take measure of our lives. It ensures that we are using our one short life in a way that is worthy of the gift.

There are so many ways to measure our lives. We talk a lot about success, but everyone has a different definition. We talk about the importance of family and relationships, but how does one measure these. What measuring stick do you use to assess your life? Career? Money? Status? Stuff? Education? Popularity? Integrity? Happiness? Adventure? Health?

At different points in our lives, we all use some of these to measure our lives, but over time most of us move on to things that are harder to measure. How many people love you? Do you love what you do? Do you feel like you are doing what you were born to do? How many other people have you helped to become successful, happy, educated? How many lives have you improved? How long will you be remembered after you die? Are you at peace with God?

These are enormous questions, but we should not let that intimidate us. How do you measure your life? What do you look for when deciding if you are on the right path? How do you judge your progress?

One of the most famous alumni from my high school is Thomas Keneally, the author of *Schindler's Ark*, which was later made into the movie *Schindler's List*. He spoke at my graduation and told the story of how he came to write the book. He was in New York and visiting a leather goods store. As he looked at some briefcases, the proprietor struck up a conversation with him. Before long the conversation came upon two questions that changed Keneally's life forever.

"What do you do?" the store owner asked.

"I'm a writer," Keneally responded.

"What are you writing?" was the second question.

"Well, to be honest, I'm struggling right now. Not sure what I am going to write next."

The proprietor put the briefcase he was holding back on the shelf, straightened up, looked deep into Keneally's eyes, and said, "Come back tomorrow morning and I will tell you a story."

The next morning, Keneally returned to the store, and for the rest of the day listened to the most captivating true story. The owner of the store was Poldek Pfefferberg, a Holocaust survivor thanks to Schindler. Pfefferberg was in possession of the original list along with a vast collection of files and documents relating to Oskar Schindler.

It's one of those moments that puts a chill up my spine every time I think about it, a moment that was dripping with destiny. All Thomas Keneally did was walk into a leather goods store with a case of writer's block.

The book went on to become the defining work of Keneally's life, and together with Steven Spielberg's movie adaptation, it raised awareness of the Holocaust among younger generations.

Twenty years later, I was walking along the beach in Sydney. Glancing ahead, I saw Thomas Keneally walking toward me. We spoke for a few minutes, and I asked him how the extensive research he did for the book had affected him. He shared with me his experience of meeting people who had been taken in by strangers and hidden from the Nazis. "Their stories were chilling. Everything was at stake at every moment" he explained, and then paused before continuing, "I still wake up some nights, short of breath and sweating. In the dream someone was hiding me, we had been discovered, and myself and the people who were hiding me were about to be executed. That's when I wake up in the dream... at the same place every time."

There was something about the way he described hiding and being hidden that got my mind turning. I started researching the different times in history people needed to be hidden from their persecutors. It has happened over and over throughout history. Innocent people, hidden, often by strangers, from a tyrannical and brutal adversary, at great personal risk. The persecuted have always found a few brave men and women willing to hide them.

Now, let me ask you a question. If you were in trouble, being hunted unjustly, how many people do you know who would risk their lives to hide you?

A Polish Holocaust survivor once told Warren Buffet, "Warren, I'm very slow to make friends, because when I look at people, the question I ask is: Would they hide me?"

There is no perfect way to measure our lives. But these two questions add another layer that is worth considering: How many people would hide you? How many people would you be willing to hide?

Remember.

We remember at funerals. Why do we wait? It is so important to take a little time to remember each day. It's important to remember our own story, and it's important to remember the story of our relationships. Don't wait for tragedy to strike to remember.

There are some essential truths that are critical to remember: *You matter. You are loved. You are of great value.* But we forget.

I tell my children each night, "No matter what, no matter when, no matter where, Daddy always loves you." I never want them to forget. If I tell them occasionally, they will remember during the good times, but I want them to remember when they are confused and afraid, when their lives are turned upside down.

It's important to remember your story. You have been through tough times before and you weathered the storm. You have had many wonderful experiences in life. You have so much to be grateful for. But we forget.

It's important to remember the story of your primary relationship. If I sit down for fifteen minutes, look at photos of the life I share with my wife, think about the highs and the lows, it gives perspective to whatever our relationship is preoccupied with right now. This simple exercise makes me a better husband. There is something about our story that reminds me to pay attention.

It's important to remember your children's stories and to help them remember too. I love showing my children photos and videos of them when they were younger. I love telling them stories about their childhood. Remembering their stories makes me a better father too.

Over time, they become curious about my life. It's a magical day the day they ask, "Tell me about when you were a little boy, Dad." I say to them: Pick a number and I will tell you all about my life when I was that age. They love it. They are fascinated.

A person who forgets his or her story goes mad. Couples who forget their stories become impatient and grow apart. Parents and children who forget their story lose their tenderness. And a society that forgets its story is doomed to make the same mistakes all over again. Take time to remember.

Peace, serenity, and tranquility.

There is so little peace, serenity, and tranquility in the world today. We have made the world so busy, noisy, anxious, and violent that peace, serenity, and tranquility can seem unattainable. Perhaps that's why we don't talk about them, teach about them, or strive for them. But surely, they deserve a place in the curriculum of life.

Think about times in your life when you experienced tranquility. What was different? Take note of who and what steals away your peace. Is it worth it? Try to be aware of what disturbs your serenity. If you can locate the source of these disturbances, awareness will lead you to choose serenity.

One of the most famous prayers in history is called the Serenity Prayer. It was written by Reinhold Niebuhr and has been practiced by men and women of all faiths, and there is genius is its simplicity.

Pray this prayer once an hour for an entire day, from when you wake to just before you go to bed at night. Observe yourself throughout the day. Before you go to sleep that night, reflect on how praying for thirty seconds each hour changed the way you experienced life that day. You will be amazed.

God,
Grant me the serenity to accept the things I cannot change,
the courage to change the things I can,
and the wisdom to know the difference.
Amen.

Begin to build a life that is conducive to peace, serenity, and tranquility. Make choices that invite peace into your life.

Words have power. There were certain words and phrases that my parents wouldn't tolerate in our home when we were growing up. There was a long list. Idiot was one, shut-up was another, and of course, the F-word. If one of these words of phrases was used the person would be sanctioned, but there was always an explanation. Reason was given for why we didn't use those words and phrases. "Your father and I are not raising idiots," I can still hear my mother saying. As I child I was always surprised how harsh the penalty was for telling someone to shut-up. My parents explained repeatedly that it was exceedingly disrespectful to deny a person their voice in any situation. I remember the first time one of my brothers used the F-word. I will never forget what my father said to my brother. "That's an angry word, isn't it? If you use angry words, you will become an angry man. I love you too much for that. It's okay to get angry, we all get angry from time to time, but learn to express your anger in healthy and constructive ways. Words like that don't mean anything, so it is impossible for anyone to understand your anger."

Some words are angry, others are harsh, some are firm, others are weak or neutral. These three words are beautiful: *peace, serenity, and tranquility.* Say them quietly aloud, over and over, for two minutes. Take note of how these words make you feel. You will be amazed how just saying these beautiful words invites them into the depths of your being. Invite peace, serenity, and tranquility into your life.

The central question.

In the beginning, I proposed a question: Can someone who has been broken be healed and become more beautiful and more lovable than ever before?

Life's biggest questions need to be personalized to a particular person. What's the meaning of life? is a question that has been pondered by lovers of wisdom for thousands of years. But the question that really matters to you is: What is the meaning of *your* life?

So it is with the central question of our journey together: Can someone who has been broken be healed and become more beautiful and more lovable than ever before?

Theoretically, most of us can probably concede that this is possible. But I am little concerned with theoretical inquiry. I don't write to prove or disprove theories. I don't write for an audience of many. I write for you, the reader. One, real, living, breathing human being, who is trying to make sense of life. Not life in general, but your own life.

I hope that what I have shared in these pages has led you to a healthier relationship with your own brokenness, and I hope you are on your way to believing that *you* can be healed and become more beautiful and more loveable than ever before.

The mountaintop.

Every life has highs and lows. I've had more than my fair share of mountaintop experiences, but like everyone else, I live in the valleys and on the plains.

The thing that surprises me in this moment is the stillness in my soul. Writing this book has been a tumultuous experience. I have experienced the effortless grace of inspiration over the years as a writer, but this book wasn't like that. These words didn't come from a mountaintop experience. A high price had to be paid for them. They were hard-fought for in the lowlands and the wastelands.

I know there will be more storms, and I know I am better prepared than ever before. But right now, in this place, at this time, I cherish this profound calmness. It is a gift.

There is so much more I would like to share with you. I sit here, paging through my journals, and on each page, I find some insight that begs not to be left out. Here are some that I cannot pass over.

1. You cannot live a meaningful life by filling your life with meaningless things and activities.

2. Everyone is going to hurt you. Find the ones that are worth the suffering and heartache, don't let anyone harden your heart, and remember, that even with your best efforts to avoid it, you are going to hurt people too.

3. Don't complain. It's not attractive or productive.

4. Give people the benefit of the doubt. Life is difficult and messy, and everyone is carrying a heavy burden.

5. Death comes to us all. When death approaches, the person you have become meets the person you could have been. This is a humbling encounter. Don't wait for it. Meet with the person you are capable of becoming for a few minutes each day. The more time you spend in these meetings the less you will fear death. Use your thoughts, words, choices, and actions, to close the gap between who you are today and who you are capable of being. This is the path that leads to a deeply fulfilling life.

6. Ignore your critics. Everyone has them. They will tear down in an hour what they couldn't build in a lifetime. But life eventually puts all critics in their place. With time they become remote and unimportant. The people who love you don't care about what your critics care about; they care about you as a human being. Your critics don't see you as a human being. They have dehumanized you. They see something in you that unsettles something in them. So, they have to decide: attack you or investigate

their own dark mystery. Most people don't know you well enough to compliment you or criticize you, and it is the unseen moments of our lives that define us.

The good life.

Since Aristotle first spoke of "the good life" almost 2,500 years ago, it seems everyone has been on a quest to experience it. I have heard many people speak about it and I have read many books on the subject. Some people think it's about success and accomplishment. Others think it's about money and things. Some think it's about love and family. Others think it's about food, wine, travel, adventure, education, meaningful work, independence, friendship, and pleasure.

There's nothing wrong with these things, unless these things are all you've got. Because even all of these things together will not deliver the good life.

There is only one ingredient essential to the good life. So essential that without it, the good life is impossible. You would think that such an ingredient would be widely sought after. It isn't. You might think that such an ingredient is scarce. It isn't. You may think this ingredient is expensive. It isn't. You may think people would be clamoring to get their hands on it. They aren't.

When people talk about the good life, you get the impression that it is mysterious and only available to a select few people. This isn't true.

There is no secret to the good life. It isn't a mystery. No exceptional talent is required. It isn't only for the rich and famous. It is available to everyone, everywhere, at all times.

What is the essential ingredient of the good life? Goodness itself. The secret to the so-called good life has always been right before our very eyes. If you wish to live the good life, fill your life with goodness. Fill your life with love, kindness, gratitude, compassion, and generosity.

Take risks with your goodness. Test the limits of your goodness. Don't just love, astonish people with your love. Don't just dabble in generosity, live a life of staggering generosity.

How would your life change if your only goal was to do as much good as possible? Let's find out. Don't let this question remain unanswered. Celebrate goodness every chance you get.

Don't waste your gold dust.

I hope you enjoyed

life is *Messy*

It is a privilege to write for you.
I hope it nourished you
in the ways you needed to be fed
at this time in your life.

Matthew Kelly

Subscribe to **Matthew's YouTube Channel**
to experience the *Life Is Messy* Video Series.

 YouTube

www.youtube.com/matthewkellyauthor

Visit **MatthewKelly.com** for his Blog
and so much more.

ABOUT THE AUTHOR

Matthew Kelly is a best-selling author, speaker, thought leader, entrepreneur, consultant, spiritual leader, and innovator.

He has dedicated his life to helping people and organizations become the-best-version-of-themselves. Born in Sydney, Australia, he began speaking and writing in his late teens while he was attending business school. Since that time, 5 million people have attended his seminars and presentations in more than 50 countries.

Today, Kelly is an internationally acclaimed speaker, author, and business consultant. His books have been published in more than 30 languages, have appeared on the *New York Times*, *Wall Street Journal*, and *USA Today* bestseller lists, and have sold more than 45 million copies.

In his early-twenties he developed "the-best-version-of-yourself" concept and has been sharing it in every arena of life for more than twenty-five years. It is quoted by presidents and celebrities, athletes and their coaches, business leaders and innovators, though perhaps it is never more powerfully quoted than when a mother or father asks a child, "Will that help you become the-best-version-of-yourself?"

Kelly's personal interests include golf, music, art, literature, investing, spirituality, and spending time with his wife, Meggie, and their children Walter, Isabel, Harry, Ralph, and Simon.